CENTRAL

Ultimate USP

is You

■

The Ultimate USP is You

Proven techniques for Sales Success

■

JIM COWDEN

the Institute of Management

FOUNDATION

PITMAN PUBLISHING

PITMAN PUBLISHING
128 Long Acre, London WC2E 9AN

A Division of Longman Group Limited

First published in Great Britain 1994

© Jim Cowden, 1994

British Library Cataloguing in Publication Data
A CIP catalogue record for this book can be obtained
from the British Library.

ISBN 0 273 60617 4

1 3 5 7 9 10 8 6 4 2

Typeset by PanTek Arts, Maidstone.
Printed and bound in Great Britain by Bell and Bain Ltd, Glasgow.

The Publishers' policy is to use paper manufactured
from sustainable forests

Contents

■

Introduction

∎

Over the years, there have been a great many books written on the subject of selling and sales. However, my experience has been that they all concentrate on the WHAT of selling. I have yet to read a book which gave any in depth understanding of the HOW of selling.

This book includes many of the WHATS but has been written to redress the balance by concentrating on the HOWS.

The reason the book is called *The Ultimate USP is You* will become clear at the end of this introduction. It is subtitled *Proven Techniques for Sales Success*, because this book is based on a sales training programme which has been used for many years in almost every type of selling situation you can imagine. Whenever it has been used, measurement criteria have been put in place which have proven that the training has brought about a significant improvement in sales results and performance.

The book is laid out so that much of it can either be read in its entirety or used as a working manual. There are areas, however, where your input is essential in 'customising' it to your own selling environment.

During the course of reading this book you will become exposed to 'jargon', much of which is standard for those people already employed in the selling profession. However, to make life as simple as possible, all of this is explained within the text.

I have written this book to provide a framework to allow you to think about the process and practice of selling, but inevitably it is peppered with anecdotes and examples from real life situations in an attempt to further clarify your understanding. I would also point out that during my career, either as a sales person or a Sales Trainer, I have never been involved in any of the industries which have attracted bad press coverage, for example Time Share, nor have I ever considered any of the industries with which I was involved to be 'high pressure', although I have been active in financial services (insurance and investments), double glazing, home improvements and directory advertising. In addition to these, I have also worked with banks, computer companies, pharmaceutical companies etc., where the sales practice can stand intense scrutiny without fear of adverse criticism.

If there has been any pressure in my selling career, it has been self-imposed and the only person under pressure was me. I have never needed nor wanted to put the customer under pressure.

In all of these instances I have applied the selling skills covered in this book and have a conscious desire to present selling as an ethical profession, which is what it is.

The selling profession sometimes attracts unfortunate attention, even outside of some of the more dubious areas referred to before, with the result that many sales people are referred to – unjustifiably – as 'con men'. These are interesting words because their derivation is 'confidence men' implying that good sales people inspire confidence and so they should, but thereafter the line of substantial difference between 'con men' in the accepted sense of that expression and professional sales people should be drawn.

Selling is such an important profession that it deserves a better reputation than it attracts and indeed it is the **Oldest Profession.**

Whenever I pose the question; 'What is the Oldest Profession?', I am invariably met with the reply, 'Prostitution'. This isn't true, **Selling is the Oldest Profession**, because if it wasn't being sold it wouldn't be prostitution, it would merely be 'enthusiastic amateurism'.

Don't let anybody ever forget that in terms of the bottom line

NOTHING HAPPENS TILL SOMEBODY
SELLS SOMETHING.

Some of you will read this book and your expectations may be raised that you will be transformed from the proverbial 'shrinking violet' into a vibrant, exciting, competent and confident sales person. Be aware that this may not be the case. In much the same way that Computer Programmers are born **then made**, so are sales people. You need the basic aptitude and personality for the profession first. Some of you will not become sales people and if the only thing that this book does for you is convince you of that, it will truly have been an investment.

The selling business can be a tough business; don't make it harder by trying to turn water into wine. I have met too many emotional and psychological casualties to encourage that to happen again.

Finally, if some of the references and anecdotes in this book are found to be humorous, this should in no way detract from the seriousness of the messages, but will serve to remind you that: **Selling can be a fun business too.**

I have tried as far as possible to ensure that any re-marks are 'non-sexist', but there may be occasions when in relating experiences I have had to fall back on the gender which applied in that situation.

The ultimate USP

The only reason that any company would develop or invent a **Unique Selling Point** for a product or service would be to create a SUSTAINABLE COMPETITIVE ADVANTAGE over its competitors.

In Appendix B of Chapter 1 I will explain to you how USPs are few and far between and where they do exist their uniqueness isn't usually very long-lived.

There are a few very simple reasons why this is so:

- competitors can eventually copy your products or services
- they can copy your pricing structure
- they can copy the way you advertise, promote and market your products
- they can copy the way you distribute your products
- they can even copy your product development ideas
- they CANNOT copy people!

The ONLY SUSTAINABLE COMPETITIVE ADVANTAGE a company can have is PEOPLE with the ability to CREATE, ANTICIPATE and REACT to CHANGE quicker and better than the competition.

Therefore: THE ULTIMATE USP IS YOU!

I hope you will learn from this book and when you have, I wish you GOOD HUNTING and GOOD FARMING and GOOD PROSPECTING and GOOD SELLING and GOOD LUCK.

ON A WALL IN ZURICH

When I began writing this book, I originally used the working title, *Face-to-Face,* as the book deals with face- to-face selling skills. However, as there are other books which use that title, although they deal with different subject matter, I had to think again.

In the summer of 1993 I was on a visit to Zurich for a meeting with my client of many years, Robin Terrell of Ciba Vision, during which I noticed that on his wall was the quotation, 'The Only Sustainable Competitive Advantage ...'. I had created this 'declaration' when working with Robin and his management group in the UK several years before and the importance of the statement had obviously meant a great deal to him.

It seems appropriate that a person who figures so prominently in this book, as he has done in my career, should unwittingly have given me the title.

1

The thinking sales person

Most people become involved in the sales profession without ever giving the process of selling any real thought.

Yet my experience of working with some of the top sales people in the world has been that they are the ones who have spent time in a great deal of thought, much of it original, about the actual process which takes place.

So let's think about selling.

What is selling?

At this point I would invite you to write as many creative definitions as you can. The working definition which we will use is printed below, complete with an explanation.

WHAT IS SELLING?

Selling is: **motivating** the **customer** or **prospect** to **buy** what **you** have to **offer**.

In this context I refer to **motivation** quite simply as: 'A **personal** reason for doing something'.

In layman's terms, selling is about discovering the reason why the person to whom you are talking will part with money for the product or service which you have to offer.

Why do people buy anything?

There are only two reasons why anyone buys anything, possibly three if you combine reasons one and two.

1   NEED

2   DESIRE

3   a combination of NEED and DESIRE.

NEED

Need is probably the most commonly quoted reason why people buy things. In a commercial environment, most people buy on the basis of need, because in the main the purchase of your products or services will solve problems which they have or provide opportunities which would otherwise be unavailable to them.

Indeed, in many commercial situations the products or services being purchased are in fact 'sold on' to your customers' customers. While this may be a driving force in this situation, most successful salespeople also discover a '**desire**', i.e., a reason why the prospect **wants** to buy the product or service.

DESIRE

Desire is the reason why people want to buy things.

In a domestic environment, most people buy on **desire** and not on **need**.

A couple of examples:

1   most private individuals who buy shares of companies do so because they **want** to generate an income either now or at some future date, or they **want** to see their capital grow, or both. They do **not need** to buy shares.

2   people who buy double glazing do not, in the main, **need** double glazing. In the case of **need** (rotting windows etc.), single ordinary glazing would suffice and is invariably less expensive. They **want** to buy double glazing for any number of reasons, including:

2

- heat retention
- sound insulation
- improvement of property value
- increasing the desirability of their property when selling, etc.

In fact there will often be situations in the domestic environment where the prospective customer needs a product or service, but finds that the purchase of this is in conflict with something which they want to buy.

In the vast majority of these situations, the purchase made will be the one based on desire.

I was involved in just such a case where the prospect, according to all of the rules which apply in that industry, needed to buy life insurance. In fact the prospect accepted and agreed that this was the case. However, at that time the prospect wanted to buy a new car. The purchase made was the car and the life insurance was left until another day.

However idiosyncratic that may appear, you always have to bear in mind that a great deal of emotion can be involved in the buying process.

Now that we have begun to understand why people buy things, it is appropriate to understand the buyer/seller relationship:

3

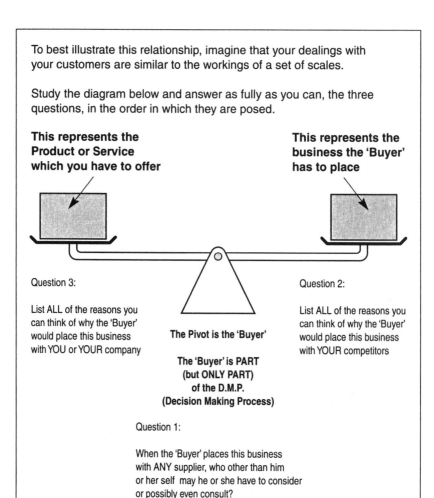

To best illustrate this relationship, imagine that your dealings with your customers are similar to the workings of a set of scales.

Study the diagram below and answer as fully as you can, the three questions, in the order in which they are posed.

This represents the Product or Service which you have to offer

This represents the business the 'Buyer' has to place

Question 3:

List ALL of the reasons you can think of why the 'Buyer' would place this business with YOU or YOUR company

The Pivot is the 'Buyer'

The 'Buyer' is PART (but ONLY PART) of the D.M.P. (Decision Making Process)

Question 2:

List ALL of the reasons you can think of why the 'Buyer' would place this business with YOUR competitors

Question 1:

When the 'Buyer' places this business with ANY supplier, who other than him or her self may he or she have to consider or possibly even consult?

Fig 1.1 The Buyer/Seller Relationship

Below, you will find many of the answers which you have written, but perhaps not all, as these will vary depending on your industry and your experience.

The ones which do appear are the answers taken from hundreds of sales people over many years.

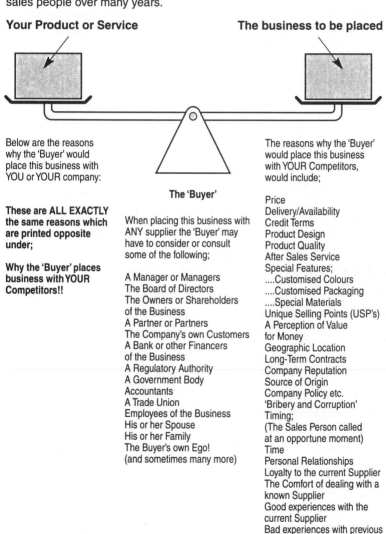

Your Product or Service

The business to be placed

The 'Buyer'

Below are the reasons why the 'Buyer' would place this business with YOU or YOUR company:

These are ALL EXACTLY the same reasons which are printed opposite under;

Why the 'Buyer' places business with YOUR Competitors!!

When placing this business with ANY supplier the 'Buyer' may have to consider or consult some of the following;

A Manager or Managers
The Board of Directors
The Owners or Shareholders of the Business
A Partner or Partners
The Company's own Customers
A Bank or other Financers of the Business
A Regulatory Authority
A Government Body
Accountants
A Trade Union
Employees of the Business
His or her Spouse
His or her Family
The Buyer's own Ego!
(and sometimes many more)

The reasons why the 'Buyer' would place this business with YOUR Competitors, would include;

Price
Delivery/Availability
Credit Terms
Product Design
Product Quality
After Sales Service
Special Features;
....Customised Colours
....Customised Packaging
....Special Materials
Unique Selling Points (USP's)
A Perception of Value for Money
Geographic Location
Long-Term Contracts
Company Reputation
Source of Origin
Company Policy etc.
'Bribery and Corruption'
Timing;
(The Sales Person called at an opportune moment)
Time
Personal Relationships
Loyalty to the current Supplier
The Comfort of dealing with a known Supplier
Good experiences with the current Supplier
Bad experiences with previous Suppliers

5

Fig 1.2 The Buyer/Seller Relationship

Appendix A

Understanding the buyer/seller relationship

QUESTION 1

The 'buyer' may have to consider or consult:

A manager or managers

Perhaps you are working quite far down the decision- making process (DMP); perhaps you have no choice. If possible, try to meet the 'buyer' further up the company ladder.

The Board of Directors

This could be an improvement on the last situation, but does your product or service lend itself to getting to the board? If it does, try to get in front of them.

The Owners or Shareholders of the Business

In a private company you may be able to get to these; in a public corporation be aware that everyone knows that they are ultimately answerable to these people.

A partner or partners

In this situation, you are at least talking to a partner, but which of them is the more/most senior?

The company's own customers

If your product or service is being 'sold on' this will be a major consideration. You probably can't influence it but need to be conscious of the fact. However, don't let your 'buyer' use this as an excuse.

A bank or other financers of the business

You will probably never know if this is the case, but if your product or service involves major capital expenditure, it could be an influencing factor. However, in most cases, the product or service will have to be bought from someone, so don't be put off.

A regulatory authority

This is a classic situation in industries like pharmaceuticals which need a product licence from government health departments in order to operate. If this applies in your business you should already know and be taking this into consideration.

A government body

Common practice in areas such as exporting, but could also apply in home improvements where planning permission is required from local government.

Accountants

7

This is quite a common 'put off' excuse in the financial services industry, but there will be times when it is genuine and you will even find occasions when a customer wants to proceed with a purchase to take advantage of a financial year-end or some other tax advantageous situation. There is one real danger in this situation, however, if you are in the financial services industry; most accountants and lawyers have agencies for financial services products which will compete with what you are selling so you could lose out on the basis that someone else has a vested interest.

A trade union

Don't underestimate this situation, I once worked with a thread manufacturer who sold to a clothing factory. Because of the system of bonus payments in the clothing factory a high 'breakage rate' on the thread would have affected these bonuses. The trade union was an important part of the DMP.

Employees of the business

In an ever-increasing number of situations, companies will take their employees' thoughts into consideration when purchasing such diverse items as: vending machines, catering services, typewriters, word processors, computer software, office furniture, company cars, etc.

The buyer's spouse

Insurance sales people will always try to get both members of the family together, because they are both directly involved. The wife may choose the new fitted kitchen; the husband will usually have to contribute towards the cost.

I worked with a motor manufacturer of executive cars who had a standard rule: irrespective of the importance of the businessman, if the new car purchase is being financed from the domestic budget, make sure you get the wife as well – she has a bigger say than you might think.

They, not I, also added: the wife will also change the colour!

The buyer's family

Think about holidays, televisions, video film hire, computer games, video and hi-fi – the children have an enormous vote.

The buyer's own ego!

As well as wanting to satisfy themselves that they have done the best possible deal for their own company, many buyers will want to feel that they have positively 'got one over on you'. Failure to positively stroke the ego in these situations could cost you the business. The real trick is to leave them feeling that they have won in the bargaining when they haven't – **but don't tell them**!

Appendix B

Understanding the buyer/seller relationship

QUESTIONS 2 AND 3 COMBINED

Before expanding upon the answers in the diagrams, I am working on the assumption, however dangerous, that to be in competition there is a large degree of similarity between your product and your competitor's, otherwise they probably wouldn't be competitors.

Why the 'buyer' places the business with your competitors or with you and your company

These fall into three distinct categories:

- **Category 1** Reasons which are entirely based on the product or service which you are selling.
- **Category 2** Reasons which are based in part on the product or service, but are also based on the company which is supplying.
- **Category 3** Reasons which have little or nothing to do with the product or service, but tend to be more emotional and consequently often more difficult to overcome in a competitive situation.

CATEGORY 1

Price and Credit Terms

In the vast majority of situations you can match your competitor's price and credit terms.

Delivery/availability

You can either deliver on time or have the product available at the required time – or you can't. However, check what the required time is. Many sales people 'hang' themselves with delivery promises which they find difficult to keep and which the customer may not need.

Product Design

To be in serious contention, your product design is already what is required, so hang on in there.

Product Quality

If your product quality is not as good as your competitor's, it usually means that the 'buyer' doesn't need the high specification that is currently being supplied, or you wouldn't be in contention. If this is the case it should give you a price advantage. In most cases the product quality will be 'on a par' with the competition.

After Sales Service

If your company doesn't have it – **get it**!

Special Features: Customised colours

If you want the business, offer the service, like: manufacturers of football outfits, commercial vehicles and cars, window awnings and blinds, corporate give-aways (pens, notepads, etc.), diaries, PVC binders, etc.

Customised Packaging

An intrinsic part of 'own label' goods, etc.

Special Materials

Materials for fire resistance, special grades of stainless steel for the food industry, etc.

Unique Selling Points (USPs)

There are very few of these left and, where they exist, their sustainable uniqueness isn't usually very long-lived.

Examples are plain paper copiers – until the 1970s the USP of Xerox. 'Goretex' – the breathing synthetic fabric for outdoor wear, the USP of WL Gore, now being emulated by many other manufacturers. The 'safety cage' in motor cars, once the USP of Volvo – but not any more!

A Perception of Value for Money

All people buy on this perception; your job is to convince the customer that it exists in your product.

Tom Peters, *the* management 'guru' of the 1980s and 90s, said: '**Sometimes Perception is all there is.**'

CATEGORY 2

Geographic Location

11

Some 'buyers' prefer to deal with local companies – some don't. It will work **for** you as often as it works **against** you.

Long-Term Contracts

Sometimes customers get locked into long-term contracts to gain a price advantage, (perhaps this is only a perception – see above), sometimes because of warranty conditions, etc. Don't let the 'buyer' use this as an excuse.

You can sell on the same basis, or you can follow the example of Xerox in the early 1970s whose copiers were only on short-term contracts. They used this as a powerful argument against customers being 'locked in' to agreements which didn't allow them the freedom to change with improving technology. My personal belief is that a contributor to the Xerox 'problems' of the mid- and late '70s was the abandonment of this practice. As an ex-Xerox man myself, I'm glad to say that these appear to have long since been overcome.

One major computer manufacturer in the 1990s has adopted the practice of not 'locking in' their customers with great effect.

Company Reputation

I know people who will only buy computers from IBM, because of that company's reputation, irrespective of the relative cost. Your company has a reputation too – make sure it's a good one – and don't ever forget that you are a significant part of that reputation.

Source of Origin

Arab countries won't buy goods of Israeli origin. In some areas of the UK, Jewish people still won't buy German cars. I know of one publican who, having fought in World War II in Burma, wouldn't knowingly buy Japanese goods.

Company Policy

There may be a company policy in place which prevents you from selling to the prospective customer, but this is extremely unusual, unless it fits into the 'source of origin' category. However, check that this is a real objection and not an excuse, for example, some companies in the UK say that they have a policy of only buying British cars.

This is a real corker!

Consider the situation in the motor car industry in the UK: Ford – American parent company, with a significant proportion of their range being manufactured in other European countries; Vauxhall (General Motors) – American parent company, with the same situation regarding parts of their range.

What about that great British Institution, Rover? Owned by BMW of Germany and, at the time of writing, Honda of Japan.

Does the fact that Nissan cars are sometimes made in the UK make them any less Japanese?

I'm sure that there are companies in other European countries who appear to espouse the same type of xenophobic attitude, for example, Seat of Spain and Skoda of the Czech Republic, both owned by Volkswagen of Germany.

You would be amazed if you knew how much of the Scotch whisky industry is owned by American, Canadian, Japanese and English companies!

If this is the only reason why someone won't buy what you have to offer, there is something else you've done wrong or haven't found out, because this excuse doesn't hold water.

CATEGORY 3

'Bribery and Corruption'

It isn't widespread, but it exists. DON'T GET INVOLVED! However, if you want to be involved in this type of practice, the advice offered in this book will be an absolute waste of your time.

Timing (the sales person called at an opportune moment)

13

Sometimes this can be a matter of **good luck**. You will often find that this lucky sales person has a habit of making more calls more often than the others. This sales person will also keep an eye open for what is happening in his or her area. New businesses, construction sites, businesses that are expanding, newspaper advertisements for staff, advertising features, etc.

Work harder and smarter and watch how lucky you get.

Time

To make the decision to change suppliers will often involve a great deal of time on the part of the 'buyer'.

Time to consider, time to justify to the other parts of the DMP. If you want the 'buyer' to spend this time, you will need to give him or her some very good reasons why.

Personal Relationships

'Buyers' build up relationships based on trust with their suppliers. You will need to be very good to make them consider ending or interrupting these relationships.

Loyalty to the current supplier

Many people think that loyalty is an out-moded concept, but this has not been my experience. Much of the basis of loyalty is due to personal relationships (see above).

The Comfort of dealing with a known supplier

Customers are people too! They like to have their comfort zones in exactly the same way as everyone else. You will need to be very good to make them prepared to step out of their comfort zone.

Good experiences with the current supplier

There are still a lot of people who believe that 'If it isn't broken, don't fix it', so even if you have the most wonderful product in the world, they will not change as long as they feel that they are being adequately supplied by their existing source.

Bad experiences with previous suppliers

In these instances, getting the customer to risk a change will not be easy. These are the converse of the people mentioned before. They have probably in the past been open to change and new ideas. One bad experience with a supplier when they have tried something new could result in them having a sub-conscious policy of never trying anything new again.

14

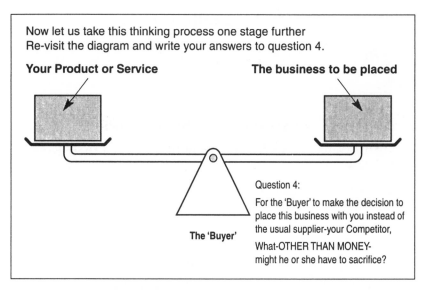

Now let us take this thinking process one stage further
Re-visit the diagram and write your answers to question 4.

Your Product or Service   **The business to be placed**

Question 4:

For the 'Buyer' to make the decision to place this business with you instead of the usual supplier-your Competitor,

The 'Buyer'

What-OTHER THAN MONEY-
might he or she have to sacrifice?

Fig 1.3 The Buyer/Seller Relationship   15

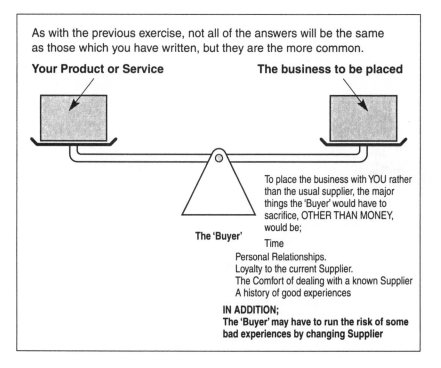

As with the previous exercise, not all of the answers will be the same as those which you have written, but they are the more common.

Your Product or Service   **The business to be placed**

To place the business with YOU rather than the usual supplier, the major things the 'Buyer' would have to sacrifice, OTHER THAN MONEY, would be;

The 'Buyer'   Time

Personal Relationships.
Loyalty to the current Supplier.
The Comfort of dealing with a known Supplier
A history of good experiences

IN ADDITION;
The 'Buyer' may have to run the risk of some
bad experiences by changing Supplier

Fig 1.4 The Buyer/Seller Relationship

Appendix C

Understanding the buyer/seller relationship

QUESTION 4

To place the business with **you** rather than the usual supplier, the major things which the 'buyer' has to sacrifice, other than money ...

The most significant fact about these is that they all fall into **Category 3**, the area of emotion. These have little or nothing to do with the product or service which you have to offer, but are nevertheless the more difficult areas to overcome. Understanding this process in the mind of the 'buyer', often subconsciously, will greatly enhance your ability to conclude a sale.

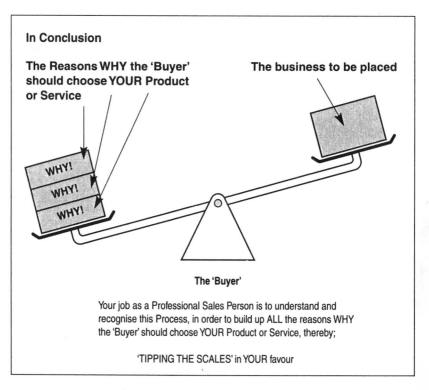

Fig 1.5 The Buyer/Seller Relationship

Remember – it may not be enough that the Customer **needs** what you have – **you** may have to get the Customer to **want** it!

When is a customer a client?

This is not simply a case of semantics, there is a distinct difference. Unfortunately there is a tendency to use the word client as an up-market expression for a customer.

A **customer** is someone who buys from you, whereas a **client** is someone who seeks your **professional advice** (even when they know that the probable outcome is that they will buy from you on the basis of that advice).

Many of you reading this book will be in businesses where you will always have customers and not clients. However, if you have customers who can become clients you could effectively 'lock out' most of your competition.

17

In working with sales people from the Insurance Industry, who are prone to referring to customers as clients, I have always told them that the first time they approach someone who buys from them they are dealing with a customer. This may be true of the second or even the third time. However, after a while, the customer will base decisions on their professional advice. At that point, the customers become clients. These insurance sales people also found a major difference between a customer and a client; **the client calls you!**

Think about the Power of that!!

Another interesting thing about clients is that they come to trust your judgement – until it proves to be 'suspect'. Imagine the situation where a client comes to you to ask for advice about something relating to the type of product or service that you supply. In most cases, what I have seen is a sales person try to make their product or service fit the clients' needs, when in their heart of hearts they know that it quite simply doesn't provide the real answer. This is the time when you have to own up to that fact if you want to keep that client for the future. If you let him or her down now, you won't only lose a client you will also lose a customer. In my own training business I have found that when the client is seeking something which I can't deliver, the credibility I get from telling them – before they find out – is worth money in the bank.

The Customer Became a Client

It was the week leading up to Christmas 1988 when I received a telephone call from the personnel manager of Ciba Vision in Southampton.

I had been working with the parent company, Ciba Geigy, carrying out corporate training for some years and in response to an enquiry made by Ciba Vision to Ciba Geigy's head office in Macclesfield, they had been referred to me as someone who may be able to offer a solution to a particular problem which they had.

It transpired that when creating Ciba Vision in the UK, much of which was by acquisition, they were going through a programme of change over an 18-month to two-year period, which would ultimately involve the redundancy of over 50 per cent of their workforce. Their problem was that during this period they needed to ensure that production, profitability and quality targets were maintained by a workforce which knew that it would be made redundant, but didn't know when. Ciba Vision had already had talks with a firm of consultants who had proposed a solution which they were not entirely sure would deliver what they needed, hence their call to Ciba Geigy and subsequently to me.

When I received the telephone call I was asked when I could go to see the senior management team from Ciba Vision to help them, if possible, to solve their problems. On checking my diary I was able to confirm that I would be available to travel to Southampton early in February 1989. No arrangements were made other than that I would call in the new year to set up the meeting.

About ten minutes after this conversation, my telephone rang again; it was Robin Terrell, the Managing Director of Ciba Vision at that time, who referred to my previous conversation with his personnel manager and my suggestion of a February meeting and he simply asked what I was doing for the rest of that week.

As it was Tuesday of the week leading up to Christmas, my experiences in the training business were such that I had never had a customer or client who wanted to see me at that time of year, other than for a social get- together, often incorporating lunch. I did in fact have a lunch appointment the following day in Glasgow with the sales director of Terex Equipment, the earth-moving equipment division of General Motors, but I agreed to travel to Southampton on the Thursday.

To do this I had to fly to London before travelling on to Southampton and I suggested to Robin Terrell that as I had no idea where their offices were situated, he could possibly arrange to have me met at Heathrow Airport and taken on to Southampton, which he said he would try to organise. In fact later that day I received a telephone call to say that they were unable to arrange for me to be met but that they had arranged for me to collect a rented car from Avis so that I could travel from London to Southampton.

19

The first thing that struck me was that before I had even met anyone from Ciba Vision, this was a considerable sign of commitment from them.

(Let me ask you, when was the last time that a customer paid part of your expenses when you made a sales call?)

However, as planned, I travelled to Southampton on the Thursday, arriving just before lunch time. My meeting was with Robin Terrell and three of his senior management team and went on for several hours, including a working lunch, during which time I tried to identify the problems in order to recommend a solution.

As our meeting drew to a close I agreed to return to Glasgow and prepare a proposal which would outline my understanding of Ciba Vision's problems together with my recommendations. At this point Robin Terrell asked if I could fax this proposal to him before 12 o'clock noon the following day when the company was closing down for the Christmas holiday. When I asked him why he needed it by then, he replied that it was to enable him to tell the other firm of consultants whether or not he intended to use them.

My reply to this was that he should call the other firm to tell them that he would not be using them, because even if he didn't use me, he should look around until such time as he found the right solution to his problems and obviously the other firm had not provided that, otherwise he wouldn't have asked me to travel to Southampton for this meeting.

He immediately called for a ten-minute break and did exactly as I had suggested.

He had accepted my professional advice and the customer became a client!

I travelled back to Glasgow and was able to fax a 13- page proposal with recommendations, within the time agreed, and immediately after the start of 1989 this was accepted. So began an association and relationship with Robin which has been the most satisfying of my professional career and is still on-going, even though he is now Ciba Vision's Group Vice President where he operates from Bülach on the outskirts of Zurich.

CHECKLIST – CHAPTER 1

- To be really successful you will need to think about the **process of selling**.

- Place yourself in the 'buyer's' shoes and **appreciate** the things and the people that the 'buyer' has to consider;

- Who else is involved in the **DMP**? Can you get to them? If not, can you take their possible input into consideration?

- Remember that there are **three categories of reason** why the 'buyer' will buy from the competition.

- Also remember that these are all the same reasons why the 'buyer' will buy from **you**.

- Don't forget the **emotion** involved in the buyer/seller relationship.

- **Need** is often not enough; you also have to **build up** enough **reasons** why the 'buyer' should **want** to do business with you.

- **Try to turn your customers into clients.**

21

Preparing for selling

L ike many industries, selling has a language all of its own.

Features, benefits, advantages, proofs and references

Let us examine these and discover where they fit into the 'face-to-face' selling call.

A FEATURE

Any Selling Point or Fact about your Product or Service

There are some people who would describe a feature as any fact about your product, etc. Pedantically this is correct, but we are involved in the selling process, so I prefer to stick with the selling features.

I cannot imagine a situation where the fact that glass is 'a non-crystalline solid made from a fused mixture of oxides such as lime, silicon dioxide, phosphorous pentoxide, etc.' would influence the sale.

Conversely, I can visualise many situations where the following selling features of glass would influence a sale: thickness, laminated, patterned, opaque, etc.

A BENEFIT:

Something which the customer gains as a result of the feature

For example, the **safety** of **laminated** glass, the **strength** of **thick plate** glass, the **privacy** afforded by **opaque** glass or the **aesthetic appeal** of **patterned** glass.

The golden rule, however, is: A feature only provides a benefit when the customer realises that it gives him or her something. Until then it is only a feature and customers don't buy features, they buy benefits.

AN ADVANTAGE:

There are two ways of looking at these.

1   A feature of your product or service which the competition doesn't have or which is superior to that of the competition.

2   A feature of your product or service which creates an advantage for your customer over his or her competition.

PROOFS AND REFERENCES:

Sometimes you may have to 'bring your witness to court'. If you make a claim that your product or service does something, be prepared that the customer might ask you to prove it.

There are two ways:

Proof

Show results of independent tests, technical specifications from literature or submit it to the customer for trial or testing, etc.

References

Use a third party who has already tried and tested it to their satisfaction.

Beware

If you use a third party make sure that they have agreed to be used, in advance, and that their experiences have been favourable. A further danger of using third party references too loosely is that you may find that the third party, in a commercial environment, is a competitor of the customer to whom you are trying to sell.

Analysing your own products or services

To make the best possible use of this chapter you will now need to create your own lists of features, benefits, advantages and proofs and references.

Using the tables printed on the following pages as the format, take one of your products or services and list all of the selling features you can. If you have difficulty in determining whether it is a selling feature or not, list all of the features and using the glass analogy mentioned before, eliminate those which are not selling features.

25

Creating your own selling aids

You should conduct the complete exercise again on any other products or services which you have to sell. You now have sufficient information to put together a complete list of the features of your products or services which you should carry with you when visiting customers, to ensure that you always have the necessary information to hand.

Over time and with additional experience you will be able to modify the information you have by adding features, expanding on the benefits, recognising advantages you have over your competition, associating advantages for your customer based on experience of other customers in similar situations, and finally develop a comprehensive list of ways to prove the features and third party references which you can use.

The Product or Service _____

List all of the selling features of this product or service

1	
2	
3	
4	
5	
6	
7	
8	
9	
10	
11	
12	
13	
14	
15	
16	
17	
18	
19	
20	

If you are unable to list twenty don't worry, this will depend on your product or service.
It will also depend on your experience in your industry. If you're unsure, ask a colleague.
If you can identify more than twenty, continue on another page.

Fig 2.1 Features

The Product or Service _____

Make a list of the benefits which a customer would gain from these features (use the corresponding numbers).

1	
2	
3	
4	
5	
6	
7	
8	
9	
10	
11	
12	
13	
14	
15	
16	
17	
18	
19	
20	

27

If you are unable to identify the benefit which comes from the feature, ask a colleague for some help. There will be instances where you can identify more than one benefit from the feature. In these cases, modify the numbers to suit.

Fig 2.2 Benefits

The Product or Service _____

Using the same numbering sequence, re-visit your list of features and note which of these offer advantages over your competition; in so doing make a note of what these advantage are.

1	
2	
3	
4	
5	
6	
7	
8	
9	
10	
11	
12	
13	
14	
15	
16	
17	
18	
19	
20	

Not all of the features of your product or service will offer advantages over your competition. Features which give your customer an advantage over his or her competition may not be discovered until the 'face to face' meeting.

Fig 2.3 Advantages

28

The Product or Service _____

Using the same numbering sequence, re-visit your list of features and note what proof you would offer or which third party references you would use and why.

1	
2	
3	
4	
5	
6	
7	
8	
9	
10	
11	
12	
13	
14	
15	
16	
17	
18	
19	
20	

Not all of the features of your product or service will need to be proven – some will be obvious (perhaps by simply looking); for example, if you were selling computer diskettes and you stated that they were 3.5" size, it would be obvious that they were.

Fig 2.4 Proofs and references

(*N.B.* With third party references, try to vary them as you may eventually alienate customers if these are overused. You might also give the third party reference the idea that he or she is the only person using your product or service.)

How to use these selling aids

In terms of selling the real skill comes about in determining which of the features the customer will see as benefits, which of the features may be an advantage or provide an advantage, and which of the features the customer may want you to prove.

The situation which I see all too often is that where the sales person, often in desperation, simply reels off all of the features of the product or service and hopes that the customer will smile, nod or show some other sign of interest to enable the conversation to proceed down a path that will let the sales person make the sale. Or, similarly, where the sales person makes statements about the benefits of using a particular feature which the customer either doesn't recognise or doesn't feel is important in his or her situation.

The same can be said about 'spouting' advantages.

Remember the **Golden Rule**: A Feature only provides a Benefit when the customer realises that it gives him or her something.

The classic situation which I have described above is called presentation or projection selling and is anything but professional. The professional sales person takes command of the selling situation by discovering which features are of benefit to the customer, which features are advantages and which features require to be proven, by simply asking questions.

THE ADDITIONAL VALUE OF BENEFITS

As sales people you may find that one of your problems is constantly having to find new prospects to whom you can sell your products and services. If you conduct the benefits exercise as thoroughly as you can you will very soon be able to 'profile' new prospective customers, simply by asking yourself the question, 'Who needs or wants what this product gives (benefits)?'

You have now begun to identify possible new users of your products and services.

In my early career in selling people often said that I should be successful because I had 'the gift of the gab!' I was several years into selling before anybody told me about listening.

The problem is, which questions to ask. We will deal with this in Chapter 3.

HE ONLY HAD TO LISTEN!

A number of years ago I decided to improve my home by installing double glazing.

I invited a number of companies to send their sales people along to measure up the various windows and give me a quotation for the work.

Five companies did in fact appear; three didn't keep the appointments made! The first four of those who did turn up went into what I call the classic projection sell, that is, they launched into an explanation of all of the features that they could think of, hoping that at some point I would show enough interest for them to be able to 'home in' to what it was that might make me buy. On several occasions they even offered proof of their claims with the major emphasis being on how much money I would save because of the heat retention of double glazing. One or two even admitted that I would improve my heat retention for no other reason that with new windows I would cut down considerably on draughts from the existing 'old' windows.

On each and every one of these occasions, the sales person involved had to make regular breaks in their 'presentation' due to the fact that at that time I lived in the flight path of

Glasgow Airport and the noise of overhead aircraft made it difficult to sustain any reasonable conversation.

The fifth sales person to appear was the only one who used a little common sense. During the second aircraft interruption, he suddenly stopped and said to me, 'Mr Cowden, it isn't that you aren't interested in saving heat, it's more that you would like to cut down on the noise from these aircraft, isn't it?' 'Yes,' I replied, and then went on to explain to him the times of the various airplanes from the airport in the early hours of the morning during the summer months.

In no time at all he began to put together a specification of window which was more suited to noise insulation than heat retention and when he had completed that exercise, I was just as quick to put pen to paper and give him the order.

All he had to do was listen!

HE USED THE WRONG THIRD PARTY REFERENCE

Third party references can be extremely useful in business; in fact most of my own business has been built on them, but they can be extremely dangerous if abused.

In *The Field Sales Handbook* I tell part of the story concerning how I came to work with Terex Equipment who were, at the time, the earth-moving equipment division of General Motors. I had been working with a sales training company in Scotland and, when I left, the exclusion clause in my contract of employment prevented me from visiting any potential customers with whom I had contact during my time with that training company. The person who inherited my files found that one of my prospects was Terex and he duly called on them.

During his interview with the board of directors, he was asked if he or the company (I'm not sure which) had ever carried out this type of work with any other heavy engineering concerns. He replied in the affirmative and gave the name of one of the leading such companies in Scotland as the third party reference.

The weakness of this reference was that it was I who had carried out all of the work with that company and although I was prohibited from contacting them, they had contacted me on a few occasions – although I didn't carry out any work with them as a result. The person who gave the reference made the mistake, as I'm sure that many of you reading this book have also done, in thinking that it wouldn't be taken up, but it was. The managing director of Terex telephoned the training manager of the other company who told them that it really ought to be me they were contacting for this type of work.

I then received a telephone call from the Training Manager of the other engineering company, asking me to contact the MD of Terex. I knew the training manager well enough to be able to ask him to call Terex back and ask them to contact me at a specific time as I was in the middle of running a programme.

When the call came through to me and the MD introduced himself, my immediate retort was, 'I've been expecting your call and I understand you would like me to carry out some training for you!' In later chapters I will talk about 'closing the sale', but you always have to remember that you should grasp every opportunity to ask for the order. While I wasn't given a positive reply to that rather tenuous attempt to win commitment, I did manage to set up a meeting with the board.

When I arrived for that meeting, my first question to them was simple but appeared to elicit some surprise: 'Gentlemen, why do you think I am here?' The sales director, Bob Wallace, answered on behalf of the group and said, 'We have already had a presentation on training from XYZ Consultants [it would be unfair to name them], and we have come here so that you can also make a presentation to us.'

I replied by outlining the circumstances which had led up to my presence, including the telephone call from the managing director. I then quietly placed an acetate on the overhead projector which read: **You can't propose a solution until you understand the problem!**

33

I was then able to set up some meetings with various directors and senior managers of the business in order to conduct some research before submitting my proposals, at the end of which I arranged to make my presentation.

I opened the presentation meeting with the following statement, 'Gentlemen, I shouldn't be here. The reason why I am here is that XYZ Consultants want to teach your people how to sell. In the process of trying to prove to you that they are capable of doing this, they gave your managing director another company's name as a reference, which when taken up by him resulted in his being referred to me.'

The outcome of the story is that I was awarded the contract against some very stiff competition – all because he used the wrong third party reference.

CHECKLIST – CHAPTER 2

- Prepare for Selling
- Analyse your own:
    - Selling features
    - Benefits
    - Both types of advantages
    - Proofs
    - References (use them don't abuse them!).
- Create your own selling aids with the analysis
- Practice using them

35

3

Getting the right information

Questioning skills

Most sales people will tell you that there are **two types of question**: **open** and **closed**. Indeed I have also heard other professionals, such as journalists, make the same statement.

They are all wrong, there are **three** types of question: two types of open question **plus** closed questions.

Let us look at these different types of question and explore the significant and extremely important differences.

The Two Types of Open Question

General Open Questions and Specific Open Questions.

General open questions are such that within the question there is **nothing to influence the answer**, whereas **Specific open questions deliberately influence the answer**.

By using open questions, the sales person will invite a great deal of information, much of which can be used at a later date.

General open questions invite this plethora of information in order to establish areas of interest which can be used to pursue the achievement of the sale.

Specific open questions are still open in order to gain a great deal of information, but they are used to pursue a particular avenue of the discussion therefore the wording of the question deliberately influences the answer. In all cases, whether general or specific, open questions will almost invariably begin with one of the following words: WHAT, WHERE, WHEN, WHY, HOW, WHICH, WHO.

Over the years, many people have quoted to me a little rhyme attributed to Rudyard Kipling which goes:

I have six honest serving men, they taught me all I knew,
Their names are What and Where and When,
and How and Why and Who.

You will see that I have given you seven, which is not my way of being pedantic, but later in this book when we discuss 'asking for the order', you will appreciate the power of WHICH in using alternatives to ask for the order.

However, back to open questions.

If I posed the general open question: WHAT is Jane Smith like? this is some of the information which I could get in reply: Jane is beautiful/tall/elegant/moody/bad tempered/strong/wilful/spoiled/brunette/intelligent/quick/alert, etc.

If, however, I posed the specific open question: WHAT does Jane Smith LOOK like? the information I would get would be influenced by the word LOOK, and would therefore be restricted to: Jane is beautiful/tall/elegant/brunette, etc. a much smaller list of possibilities.

So the major differences between the two types of open question are that while they both give more information than closed questions; the specific open question influences the answer, giving less information, but more specific information which would be appropriate in a given situation.

Let us continue by looking at closed questions and we will then return to the use of all three in the selling situation. Closed questions give short, influenced, answers, often just: YES or NO.

To continue with Jane Smith, an example of a closed question could be: is Jane Smith beautiful?

The most likely answers would be either YES or NO.

To reinforce the fact that closed questions influence the answers, we can use a closed question for each of the answers we received to the open questions:

- Is Jane Smith tall?
- Is Jane Smith moody?
- Is Jane Smith brunette?
- Is Jane Smith intelligent?
- Is Jane Smith spoiled? etc.

If you are having difficulty in opening up a question, in the early stages, try operating the principle in reverse, that is, begin with the closed question, then **convert** it to a specific open question, by beginning the question with one of the seven words. Then, finally, take out the influencing words and **convert** it to a general open question.

39

For example:

- Closed question: is the sea cold?
- Specific open question: What is the temperature of the sea?
- General open question: What is the sea like?

The answers will be similar to those below:

- Closed question: Either YES or NO
- Specific open question: The sea is **cold**, the sea is **warm**, the sea is **hot**, etc.
- General open question: The sea is cold/warm/hot/blue/green/choppy/calm/beautiful/rough/treacherous, etc.

Let's apply this thinking to a less neutral subject:

- Closed question: Is this book about selling? Answer – YES

- Specific open question: What kind of selling is this book about? Answer – this book is about the skills involved in 'face-to-face' selling.

- General open question: What is this book about? It is about selling/face-to-face selling skills/understanding the buyer – seller relationship/examining your product/understanding the selling process/making you a better sales person/ making you a thinking sales person, etc.

By now you should have begun to understand the concept behind asking the right questions and should already be practising some questions which you can apply to your own situation. The one thing that is certain is that you should be thinking about the relative values of the different types of question (see Fig 3.1).

At this point I feel it is appropriate to make a particular mention of closed questions. Almost everything I have ever read or heard about closed questions suggests that they are forbidden; this is not the case. Closed questions are vital when seeking confirmation of information, thoughts, attitudes, etc. or when looking for commitment, for example:

Closed Question

If I understand you correctly, Mr Optometrist, the majority of your patients prefer contact lenses to spectacles, is that correct?

YES confirms your thoughts, NO tells you that you have misunderstood and now have an opportunity to correct that misunderstanding.

Closed Question

Shall we go ahead and order that packaging for delivery on the first of next month?

YES, let's you know that you have the order, NO, that, at the moment, you don't have the order and there is a potential problem that you may have overlooked. It may also tell you that you asked for the order out of desperation rather than any basis of understanding.

The Product or Service _____

Using the same numbering sequence, re-visit your list of features and note below the general or specific open questions you would ask to discover whether the feature would provide a benefit to the customer.

1	
2	
3	
4	
5	
6	
7	
8	
9	
10	
11	
12	
13	
14	
15	
16	
17	
18	
19	
20	

41

Fig 3.1 Generating questions

These are both good examples of closed questions, the reason that many sales people try not to ask closed questions is that it invariably gives the customer an opportunity to say NO, the most dreaded word in the sales person's vocabulary.

But when it comes to asking for the order, there is a time when you must take the risk, or do you have to?

Later in this book you will discover ways of asking for the order which minimise that risk and you will also come to terms with the fact that Selling is a risk business, but if your control of the 'face-to-face' visit has been what it ought to be, there isn't any risk at all!

Asking questions is not the only way of getting the information from a customer which you will need in order to conclude the sale, there are OTHER INFORMATION GATHERING SKILLS.

42

Other information gathering skills

As I have said earlier in this book, I was in selling for several years before anyone told me about LISTENING. Listening is the primary skill in gaining information.

As well as listening to the facts of a situation being presented by the customer, listen to the tone of voice which will convey the feelings. Listen for the sounds of concern, despair, hope, sadness, frustration, etc. Trust me, they will all be there at some time or another.

Listening is so important that the next three pages will give you greater insight into some of the **barriers to listening**, **keys to effective listening** and some thoughts on **listening for styles**.

Barriers to listening

Be aware that while the focus of this part of the book is how these affect you, the sales person, they apply equally well to the customer.

1 Assuming in advance that the subject matter is either uninteresting, boring, trivial or unimportant.

2 Mentally criticising a speaker's way of talking or the accent, etc.

3 Focusing on mannerisms, etc.

4 Becoming over-stimulated by something that is said, leading you into a reaction before you've heard all that is to be said. This is known as the 'Yes–But' or 'Ah–But' syndrome.

5 Listening only for major facts and wanting to skip details.

6 Pretending to be attentive. People develop all sorts of behaviour to pretend that they are listening: nodding in the right places, being poised with the pen ready, etc.

7 Allowing distractions to divert your attention.

8 Allowing a speaker to continue when he or she becomes inaudible.

9 Shutting off from technical or difficult material.

10 Over-reacting to certain words or phrases.

11 Withdrawing attention and daydreaming.

43

Keys to effective listening

1 Listen optimistically – no matter how dry the subject.

2 Judge the content – not the delivery.

3 Don't jump to conclusions.

4 Listen for ideas as well as facts.

5 Work at listening and concentrate.

6 Exercise your mind – don't tune out complex material.

7 Keep an open mind and keep your emotions in check.

8 Take notes.

9 Capitalise on the fact that thought is faster than speech.

Listening for styles

Whenever a customer is speaking, he or she will give away the natural style of their thinking, for example they will use words like:

- I FEEL that this could be of value ...
- I can IMAGINE how this would help ...
- I THINK that this would work ...
- I SENSE that there would be benefit ...
- What this is TELLING me is ...
- I can ENVISAGE a situation ...
- What I'm HEARING is ...
- What I can SEE is ...

and so on.

Whatever the words are that the customer uses, note them down and, later in your presentation, USE THEM.

The customer will know that you have been listening, or if he or she doesn't know they will simply assume that you're both on the same 'wavelength'.

The end result, however, is that the customer's perception will be that you understand his or her business – a major plus in selling.

Conversely, when the customer says, 'I FEEL ...' and you reply, 'I can understand why you THINK that ...', you have a major mismatch – you haven't been listening.

What else should we listen for?

KEY WORDS AND PHRASES

The customer tells you, 'that isn't our **problem**'.

Problem is a wonderful word, because so few customers are prepared to admit that they have any, certainly not to a sales person that they may have only met half an hour before.

Ask the customer, 'What **is** the problem?'

I can't recall an occasion in the past twenty years where a customer used the word problem, when I wasn't able to conclude a sale.

Cast your mind back to the beginning of this book when I said that one of the reasons WHY PEOPLE BUY THINGS is to solve problems. In the context of a sales call it is unlikely that the customer will be thinking of a problem which is not related to the subject in hand, that is, the reason for your meeting. You only have to ask the customer what the problem is.

Another example: The customer says, 'We **should manage** with our existing equipment.' **Should manage** doesn't sound very confident to me!

Ask the customer, 'When you say you **should manage**, what could happen to prevent that?' or 'what would happen if you find that you can't?' You obviously haven't discovered the real problem yet, so keep on digging!

A further example: The customer says, 'We're **reasonably** happy **at the moment**.' There are two wonderful opportunities here. **Reasonably** sounds as unconvincing as **should**; try to get more information.

Ask the customer, 'When you say **reasonably**, how do you mean?' As an interesting aside, you will note that I have posed the question, '**How** do you mean?' This question is so grammatically incorrect as to be non-threatening, it is certainly less threatening than '**What** do you mean?' '**What** do you mean?' is the kind of question that with the wrong intonation in your voice can sound so abusive that you could be thrown out of the customer's office. I have seen it used to such effect that at best it sounded as if the sales person thought that the customer was stupid. 'How do you mean?' is so neutral that it transcends insult.

The final key phrase is, 'at the moment'. This, in my experience, is one of the most powerful buying signals a customer can ever give, if not for now, certainly at some time in the

45

future, so ask the customer: 'When you say **at the moment**, how do you see the future?'

Having looked at asking questions in response to key words and phrases, let us now look at gaining additional information based on non-verbal language, that is, BODY LANGUAGE.

I only intend to provide a few examples at the moment, because the development of our understanding of **body language** in recent years is such that I have devoted Chapter 10 to this subject on its own.

BODY LANGUAGE

In response to a Customer who is either: frowning/smiling/looking concerned/looking puzzled, etc., make the statement: 'I see that you're frowning/smiling/looking concerned/looking puzzled, etc.', and leave the statement hanging in the air, you don't have to turn it into a question.

By pausing after the statement, the customer will continue to talk, filling in the gap and explaining the reason for the frown/smile/concern/puzzlement, etc.

In a similar vein, if after a customer has replied to a question you then remain silent; in a very short time the customer will continue to speak, giving you even more information.

PAUSES AND SILENCE

Never underestimate the power of silence.

After you have asked a question, **pause**, give the customer time to think about the answer. I must, however, add the 'rider' that I would never envisage the infamous idea that this is a game where the loser speaks first. This has been put forward in the past by people who give selling a bad name.

Don't play the game – your credibility will suffer.

Later in Chapter 6, I will return to the topic of silence in more detail.

ENCOURAGING WORDS, PHRASES AND BODY LANGUAGE

Listen to someone on the telephone who isn't saying a lot but being spoken to a great deal. Ideally, if you can arrange it, listen to a teenager on the telephone (an outgoing call on your account would be ideal), and the kind of 'noises' and words you will hear will be: 'Ah?', 'Oh?', 'Yes?', 'No?', 'Uh-huh?', 'Never!', 'Well?', 'Really?', 'Mmm', 'Phew', etc.

The kind of phrases you will hear, will be: 'You're joking?', 'You don't say?', 'That's interesting', 'He/she did what?', 'He/she said what?', 'You're having me on', 'Behave yourself', 'Be serious', and many more too numerous to mention here. All of these words and phrases are greeted by a rejuvenation of the conversation flowing from the other end of the telephone.

It works exactly the same way with customers. Use them, it encourages customers to expand on what they've been saying.

In addition there are a few little body movements which achieve the same result: an enquiring look, a surprised look (often followed by an open-palmed gesture of the hands), a smile, a nod of the head, a shake of the head or even a shrug of the shoulders. I have to admit that the 'nod of the head' is one of my personal favourites. I have found that whenever I make a statement with which I would like the customer or prospect to agree, I nod my head as I make the statement. Unless they really disagree, their body language gives them away and you will also find that when you nod – they nod! Small things, but they work.

My final, for the moment, point on other information-gathering skills, is not a question, it is a statement.

47

TELL ME MORE!

Three magical words which will more often than not get you as much information as you will need to identify the opportunity to sell. I use these words on a daily basis: in the lecture room, in selling calls, in private conversation in fact everywhere. They never fail to work.

Some time ago when I was running the series of training programmes that I referred to earlier in my story about Terex, the use of these words, by me and by the participants after time, was such that the Programmes were nicknamed 'Tell me more Programmes', irrespective of the subject matter.

CHECKLIST – CHAPTER 3

- Learn to use the three different types of question

- Remember the other ways of getting information:

    - listening

    - key words and phrases

    - body language

    - pauses and silence

    - tell me more!

- Encourage the customer to keep talking

- Remember the barriers and the keys to effective listening

- Listen for the customer's style

- Generate your own questions – in advance!

49

Keeping the initiative

'Digging for gold'

I believe that you should now be in a position to put together all of the work that you carried out in the exercises in Chapters 2 and 3, along with the other information-gathering skills into an easily managed package, which will enable you to control the conversation and its direction.

Controlling the conversation and its direction

The technique is called 'Digging for Gold' because of the mental image which that creates and the interplay between your dealing with prospects and prospecting, all of which will assist you to remember the technique.

I have reproduced the whole picture on the following page, after which I will explain the various parts in detail.

'DIGGING FOR GOLD'

Let me begin by giving you a short explanation of the graphics: on the left-hand side of the page is represented a sieve, as used by gardeners and prospectors. As you move down the page more small gold nuggets appear in the sieve, based on the information you have gleaned. Beside each sieve is a spade and as you move down the page the spade becomes progressively smaller, in keeping with the lesser amount of information gained by the different types of question.

Now to the whole picture.

Get the Customer to want to answer your Questions

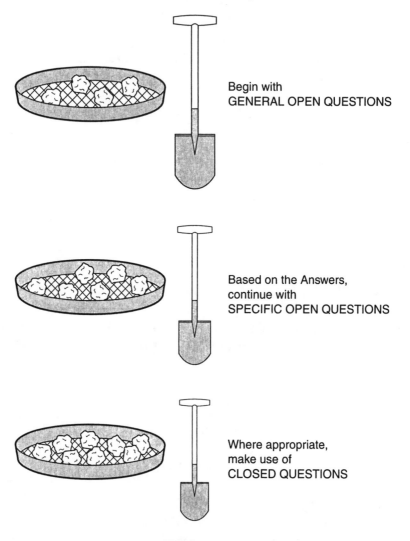

Begin with
GENERAL OPEN QUESTIONS

52

Based on the Answers,
continue with
SPECIFIC OPEN QUESTIONS

Where appropriate,
make use of
CLOSED QUESTIONS

Gather all the 'NUGGETS' together and lay them
out before the Customer in a Summary

The Final Question – 'Is There Anything Else?'

Fig 4.1 Digging for 'gold'

Getting the customer to answer questions

Stage One is to get the customer to want to answer your questions. If you don't explain to the customer that you are going to ask questions, you will eventually be met with a response similar to the following: 'Excuse me, I thought you were coming here to tell me about your product, why are you asking all of these questions?'

So get the customer prepared for the questions and wanting to answer them.

Think about your customer for a moment. If you have the right contact, for example, the decision-maker, he or she is likely to be busy so TIME is important.

To be able to make a considered decision about your product or service, the customer will want to know which part of the RANGE that you have to offer will fit into his or her business.

If the nature of your product or service is such that it involves a complete package, you will need to solicit the customer's OPINION.

Finally, I have yet to meet any reasonable person, customers included, who would refuse a plea for HELP.

So make use of all of the above, as follows:

Time

Ask, 'How much time do we have?' When you have received the reply, irrespective of how short or long that may be, ask, 'In order to make the best use of that time, do you mind if I first ask you a few questions?'

Range

Ask, 'In order to establish which part of our range would be suitable in your business, do you mind if I first ask you a few questions?'

Opinion

Ask, 'I would very much appreciate your opinion on the products which we have to offer. In order to do that would you mind if I first asked you a few questions?'

Help

Ask, 'I would really appreciate your help in finding out how our products fit into businesses like yours. To do this, do you mind if I first ask you a few questions?'

I have **never** had anyone refuse to answer questions in these situations, yet I do recall on many an occasion literally losing count of the questions I was able to ask, completely unchallenged.

My personal preference is to use the question based on TIME; it comes most naturally to me and also serves to indicate whether I have the right contact. In my business if he or she isn't busy I've got the wrong one.

Try them all, change the words to suit your own manner of speech. My words won't necessarily work for you.

THIS IS NOT A SCRIPT. Everything you read and learn in this book may have to be adapted and applied to you and your selling situation. Find out which of these works for you and use it – relentlessly, it will work.

Now that the customer is prepared to answer questions, work through the stages of 'Digging for Gold', beginning with general open questions to gain the maximum information. When you have asked enough of these to establish a direction for the conversation, continue with specific open questions, based on what you have heard.

Finally, there will be times when you need to clarify understanding or gain commitment; then you will need to ask closed questions. Don't be afraid – do it.

When you have established in your own mind that you have sufficient information to identify needs and desires which will be satisfied by your product or service, **summarise** the conversation by relaying back these 'gold nuggets'.

THE 'NUGGETS'

So what specifically are the 'gold nuggets'?

They are, first and foremost, the needs and desires expressed by the customer. They are also the words, phrases and expressions used by the customer. Remember what I said about listening. The customer will perceive that you understand his or her business if you use the language used by him or her.

You may also remember that I recommended that you take notes. In some circumstances it may be appropriate to ask the customer if that's all right. You will usually get a positive response. By taking notes you will be able to jot down the various needs and desires which you have identified as well as the customer's own manner of speech.

55

Using the whole technique naturally

My technique for taking notes was really quite simple. I reproduced sheets of notepaper with a number of little sieves drawn down the left-hand side of the page. Alongside each of these I wrote the subject to which the sieve related. For example, I knew that it was reasonable for me to ask questions about the customer's business – that created one sieve which I labelled **Business**.

I also knew that I could ask fairly safely about the history of the company and its experience of dealing with my type of product – another sieve labelled **Experiences**.

Even if it appeared a diversion I knew that I could gain some valuable information by asking about the customer himself or herself – another sieve labelled **Personal**.

Then I knew that I could ask about the company's future 'non-confidential plans' – another sieve labelled **The Future**.

I knew that I could guide the conversation round to the features of my product or service – another sieve labelled **Product**.

Finally, I knew how important it was to make a summary using the customer's own words – another sieve labelled **Words**.

When creating your own note-taking ability you will need to generate a number of general open questions to 'kick-start' the conversation. The ones on the product, however, you will already have created in the exercise in Chapter 3.

By this stage you should be in a position to give your summary, make your presentation and ask for the order, but not quite!

The final question

'Is there anything else you think I ought to know before I go on to tell you about my product?'

To this day I can recall with a fair degree of embarrassment one particular occasion when I didn't ask that question. I had got what I thought was the business from the customer and during one of my follow up calls some time later remarked on how quiet the customer's general office was.

The reason for the quietness was that many of the staff were attending a training course on a subject which I taught, but this hadn't come up in our conversation and I hadn't asked the question, 'Is There Anything Else ...?'

The $64 000 question

Let me leave this section with one question which I have used, during 'Digging for Gold' which has reaped benefits on every occasion when it has been answered directly. However, before I give you the question, I would ask you to think about the situation where you find yourself face-to-face with the customer.

If you're dealing with the right person, the chances are that he or she is busy. So why would they give up any of their valuable time to talk to you?

The only reason is that there is something they want to find out!

The question is: 'Mr(s) Customer, when you agreed to see me today, what was it that you had in the back of your mind that you wanted to know more about?' If the customer gives you a direct answer to that question, you have the overriding reason why he or she will buy. From this point on, the customer cannot fail to buy – only you can fail to sell!

'I CAN ONLY GIVE YOU TWENTY MINUTES'

I had arranged an appointment with the sales director of a large national company engaged in the manufacture and sale of fitted kitchens. On the telephone when the appointment was arranged, he had agreed to give me forty-five minutes, but when we met, I asked my normal question, 'How much time do we have?' to be told that it was only twenty minutes because he was expecting an important telephone call.

This occasionally happens, but there have been times when I felt that this was an advance excuse created by the prospective customer to bring the meeting to a premature close if there was nothing of interest for her or him in the meeting.

Invariably what happens is that the secretary has been told to call through to the office at a pre-arranged time, ostensibly with the important telephone call. Don't ask me why, but this was one of those occasions when I felt that this was what was happening.

I began by getting permission to ask questions and launched into 'Digging for Gold', aware that there was a time deadline by which I had to gain this person's interest

57

or the 'telephone call' would come through and my chance would be gone.

At precisely the twenty-minute mark the telephone rang and much to my relief I heard the sales director tell his secretary that he was in a meeting and didn't want to be disturbed, therefore would she take any further messages. By this time, the whole thing had begun to take on all the characteristics of only being a game which I was now beginning to enjoy playing.

I lost count at over sixty questions which I had asked – all of which had gone unchallenged.

After more than $1\frac{1}{2}$ hours I was able to conclude the meeting with a fairly substantial contract to train his sales people at which point he remarked, 'I look forward to you showing my people how to deal with their customers the way that you have just dealt with me. I have to admit, I like your style!'

I have had many failures in my selling career, but this one will stay with me always as one of the real successes, because I stuck to 'Digging for Gold' and made it work.

WHEN 'DIGGING FOR GOLD' DIDN'T WORK!

On the other side of the coin, there is a famous (or should I say *infamous*) occasion when 'Digging for Gold' didn't work, but as you will see, not through any fault of the technique.

Whenever I am running sales training courses, I always put my head on the 'chopping block' and demonstrate how 'Digging for Gold' should be used, a technique which I have to say is avoided like the plague by many of my competitors who don't want to run the risk of failure, thereby destroying their credibility. Perhaps their real problem is that they don't design the techniques which they teach and therefore don't have the same faith in their ability to work.

I recall a particular situation when I launched into this exercise during a training course. I had got the participants to agree to a 'neutral' product that I could sell to them and they had opted for life insurance. The two reasons why they had done so were that everybody can relate to it and their perception was that it would be a difficult thing to sell.

I gave them time to prepare for this role play with the following remit: 'Put yourself in the position in which you were before you joined this company, in terms of your personal circumstances, family, commitments, etc., together with the details of your salary and benefits etc.' In the interests of confidentiality I also told them that they could make up any salary figures they liked as the amount was unimportant and meant that they didn't need to disclose any private information to their colleagues who were present.

The one rule was that there had to be a reason why they would buy some form of life insurance and my job in 'Digging for Gold' was to uncover that reason, however obscure.

I conducted a couple of these role plays perfectly satisfactorily, taking about ten minutes for each when I decided to close with a third and final example.

I chose one of the nicest, yet quietest people in the room, and began my 'Digging for Gold'. After about ten minutes I was getting absolutely nowhere so began digging even deeper. Twenty-five minutes into the role play the other people in the room were beginning to feel uncomfortable – not that the technique wasn't working – but at the amount of personal information I was revealing as a result of having to dig deeper and deeper. Eventually, I gave up as the strain was becoming too much for everybody – including me!

I surrendered and asked the person to tell everyone what the need was that I was unable to discover. The reply that I got was that he hadn't understood that there should be a need and had written a scenario where there was absolutely no need whatsoever for any form of insurance, life or otherwise.

The moral of the story is that if you have practised 'Digging for Gold' and you know that you use it effectively, yet cannot uncover a need or desire, it probably is because there isn't one. So give up and take your activity somewhere else!

CHECKLIST – CHAPTER 4

■ Learn to use 'Digging for Gold'.

■ Prepare your general and specific open questions in advance.

■ Get the customer to want to answer your questions.

■ Adapt the concepts to suit your manner of speaking.

■ Remember always to ask the final question.

■ Use the $64,000 question.

5

Presenting solutions and creating opportunities

In Chapter 1 I told you that most people buy your products or services because they solve problems which they have or create opportunities which would otherwise be unavailable to them. The reason for reminding you of this is that solutions to problems usually stem from needs whereas opportunities are as a result of desires.

All of the sales training to which I was subjected during my career simply referred to making presentations. I would like you to remember that if you really want to succeed, you will need to remember what type of presentation it is that you should be making – based on what the customer thinks.

Making the presentation

Having satisfied yourself concerning that, the first question to ask is: When to make the presentation? Only after:

1 You have identified the customer's needs and/or desires.

2 You have summarised these for the customer.

3 The customer has agreed with your summary.

4 You have checked, 'Is there anything else?'

5 The customer is satisfied that there isn't anything else and that you have covered all of the appropriate subject matter.

The next question is: How to make the presentation? There are two aspects to this: the **verbal** and the **physical**.

Let's look at the **Verbal** first. Having identified the need or desire in your summary, you now need to select the appropriate feature(s) of your product or service which satisfy these and present them to the customer, stating the benefit(s) which will accrue as a result of the feature(s). The **sequence** is really quite straightforward: Need/Desire – Feature(s) – Benefit.

To make the whole presentation flow, however, you may want to practice linking the whole sequence with a number of pre-prepared phrases which I refer to as 'Link Phrases'. This would make the sequence look like this: Need/Desire – (Link Phrase 1) – Feature(s) – (Link Phrase 2) – Benefit.

Link phrase 1 ties the feature to the need and link phrase 2 highlights the benefit from the feature, that is, what the customer gets by buying the product or service.

Some examples of link phrase 1 would be:

1   In order to achieve this...

2   With that in mind...

3   We have developed...

Some examples of link phrase 2 would be:

1   So that you get...

2   Which gives you...

3   Which means that...

There are others that you would use according to your own manner of speech and what comes most naturally to you. If I provide a couple of examples here, you will see that the technique is anything but cumbersome and this will help you develop your own alternatives and your own style.

EXAMPLE 1 – FROM THE DOMESTIC LIFE INSURANCE INDUSTRY

'Mr and Mrs Smith, during our conversation you have been able to tell me that you want to buy a new 'dream home' involving an additional expenditure of £50 000 as well as catering for your future financial needs when you both decide to give up working. **With this in mind**, **we at** A B C Insurance **have developed** an endowment life insurance contract which is acceptable to all of the major banks and building societies as security for such a mortgage and which has a sufficiently high investment level that at the end of its term will provide you with a considerable cash surplus to be invested for your future. **This means that** you will be able to secure the extra funding necessary to buy your dream home as well as giving you the peace of mind that at the end of the time you will be in a much better position to cater for your future financial needs. In addition, in the event that either one of you does not live to the end of the period of insurance, the contract will automatically pay off the outstanding mortgage, leaving the **other with the** free title to your home, **which also gives you** the further comfort of knowing that the future financial needs of your loved ones are much more readily secured'.

This is an interesting example and I chose it for a number of reasons: even if you don't sell life insurance you can relate to having bought some, often for the purpose described in the example. The example shows how you can cover two needs or desires in one simple summary. It often isn't necessary to repeat the whole process for each and every feature.

The use of the expression 'dream home' is likely to be one that the customer used. Remember that people don't buy houses, they buy 'homes'. Because you have been able to cover two needs, you are also able to highlight two benefits – again in a simple statement. There is an opportunity to include an additional benefit that may or may not have occurred to the customer. The wording of the verbal presentation has kept away from the use of technical expressions, like:

- 'joint life first death basis'
- 'policy'
- 'collateral'
- 'pension'
- 'terminal bonus', etc.

This example uses straightforward language that the customer is likely to understand.

The wording of the presentation is such that all the way through, it concentrates on what the customer will get (benefits), for example, 'peace of mind', 'cash surplus to be invested for your future', 'the further comfort of knowing', 'financial needs of your loved ones', etc., not only benefits, but 'emotional expressions' – the ones most likely to get the customer to **want** to buy.

Finally, you may think at first that it is very long, but read it as slowly as you wish and you will find it difficult to make the presentation statement last more than a minute. The ability to do this, however, will only come with practice.

Whatever the product or service is that you sell, I am sure that you would be able to create a verbal presentation which is as 'matter of fact' as that example.

Let me give you just one more to try to reinforce the message.

EXAMPLE 2 – FROM THE CONTACT LENS INDUSTRY

'Mr Optometrist, from our conversation I understand that the vast majority of your patients need contact lenses within the range of plus "X" to minus "Y" powers and that the ability to try these lenses and supply them quickly are the things that are of greatest importance to you.

In order to give you all of this **we** at A B C Contact lenses **have devised** a total package which involves the installation of your own bank of seventy pairs of lenses in which you have defined the power parameters **which means that** you will fit the vast majority of your patients from "stock" the same day; a "fitting set" service **so that you** can try these additional lenses on the small number of patients who are outside of the usual parameters; and a next-day delivery service from our extensive stocks **so that you will offer** a comprehensive service to all of your patients.

In addition, we will operate a "top-up service" for your bank of lenses, whereby we replenish the stocks of those lenses you have sold direct from your bank to ensure that you continually have the entire range at your disposal thereby satisfying the needs of your patients.'

This is another interesting example in that it differs from the previous one because you have to repeat the sequence for each need and feature/benefit. However, despite that you will see that it is still possible to wrap the whole presentation up in a quite normal statement of the 'facts'. You may think that the example makes it too easy to provide a 'pat' answer to the problem but if you think carefully about your own products and services you may be surprised at how easy the same principle applies.

Before I move on from the verbal part of the presentation, I think it is worth adding a couple of points about the **vocal** part of that.

65

Whenever I conduct presentation skills programmes for people, whether associated with the training business, the sales presentation business or simply public speaking, I tell the participants about the different uses of the voice:

1   increased volume (not shouting) and emphasis convey enthusiasm.

2   decreased volume and 'softness' convey sincerity.

Take advantage of that when making your verbal presentation.

I recently read a quotation attributed to the late and very great Bob Paisley when he was the extremely successful manager of Liverpool FC in England: 'If you wish to be heard – speak softly!'

Let us now move on to the physical aspect of presenting solutions and creating opportunities. Many of you reading this book will make us of various visual aids, such as: brochures, technical specifications, design drawings, 'presenters' or 'sight sellers', etc.

'Presenters' and 'sight sellers' are among the names used for the folders that contain a number of clear plastic pockets into which various display type material; price lists, advertising information, brochures, photographs, references, etc., can be organised so that they may be used to support or reinforce your message during the verbal part of the presentation.

When using these, here are a few pointers that may improve the effectiveness of their usage:

1 **Don't** hand your presentation material to the customer so that he or she can take control and read through material which you either didn't intend him or her to see or which is irrelevant to the situation.

2 **Don't** hold the material over a desk to the customer and proceed to read upside down from it as you make your presentation:

   a) it creates a physical barrier between the two of you

   b) the customer now knows that you can read upside down and is beginning to worry about what was left on the desk that you may also have read.

3 **Do** take this opportunity to move alongside the customer so that you can both view it together – right way up. It breaks down the barriers between you and psychologically creates the situation where you are both on the same side looking at the 'solution to the problem'.

4 **Do** use a pen or some other type of pointer to make sure that the customer's eye is drawn to the part of the material that is relevant.

SOME ADDITIONAL POINTS

1 You need to have in-depth product knowledge in order to understand the best applications which will make customers buy.

2 The presentation should always relate to the customer's perception of the situation. That will be the real situation.

3   Make positive statements in your presentation – indicating that you assume you will get the business.

4   Make the presentation as long as it needs to be and no longer – don't waffle!

5   Remember 'Digging for Gold' and use the customer's words and phrases.

6   Make sure that the customer fully understands the benefit(s) accruing from the features(s).

7   If you have to prove the benefits – make sure you can.

8   Pre-handle likely objections (more of this in the next chapter).

9   Make sure that the customer understands and check this often.

10   Listen and watch for all the little 'buying signals'.

11   Maintain eye contact with the customer – it reinforces sincerity!

12   Use the customer's name and use it often: it helps you remember it and it improves the establishing of a 'personal' relationship.

13   KISS – It Simple, Stupid!

67

When, how and why

WHY SHOULD YOU MAKE PRESENTATIONS THIS WAY?

The summary is the real key to the presentation:

1   It helps the customer realise that you understand her or his business.

2   It helps the customer to see his or her needs clearly and all in one piece, that is, the whole picture.

3   It gives you the opportunity to use the customer's words.

THE ULTIMATE USP IS YOU

4 It allows you to highlight the customer's needs, link your features to those needs and clarify the benefits which accrue from them.

The 'Murder Kit'

I referred to the use of 'presenters' and 'sight sellers' in this section and I was recently reminded by a friend of mine that for many years I referred to these as 'The Murder Kit'. Before a professional sales person takes this piece of equipment from the briefcase to make the presentation there should be clear-cut needs and desires which make the introduction of the 'sight seller' meaningful – otherwise it shouldn't be brought out at all. In selling 'jargon' the customer is already 'dead'. That's why I call these 'The Murder Kit'.

I worked with a cosmetics company some time ago which adopted the attitude that if the sales person couldn't uncover a need or a desire then they should introduce the 'presenter' and go through this with the customer – in the hope that there was something there that may be of interest.

I personally have a few problems with this;

1 The cost of sales people is such that it would probably be as effective to mail the information and give the customers time to read it at their leisure.

2 By accepting this low quality of selling skills the companies concerned cannot really expect to create a sustainable competitive advantage.

3 The acceptance of the low quality of skills inherent in this practice gives the selling profession no credit.

4 As long as companies accept these poor standards they will get away with failure to invest in the development of their sales people – a poor prospect for ambitious sales people.

The culture of the sale

In Chapter 2 I referred to presentation selling or projection selling which is not to be confused with the making of presentations that we have just covered. Projection selling normally begins with a few perfunctory questions, followed by a whole list of features of the product or service in the desperate hope that at some point the customer will hear something of interest and ask some questions. From this point there is a great 'tennis match' between customer and sales person involving attempts to 'close the sale' from the sales person and 'objections' from the customer at the end of which, with some luck, the customer has been 'pressurised' into buying.

The sale that we are trying to develop here is entirely different. The professional sales person will make a considered and informative introduction to the customer, followed by the 'Digging for Gold' concept including getting the customer to want to answer questions. Thereafter a whole series of meaningful questions will be asked – and answered culminating in both parties understanding what the customer needs and wants (in the English language it is commonly referred to as a conversation!). This gives the sales person the opportunity to show the customer how the product or service on offer will satisfy the situation. From that point onwards objections will be minimised, but not eliminated, as we will see in the next chapter. The whole 'technique', however, is called 'empathy selling' – much more beneficial to all of the parties involved.

69

Remember the real key to selling is to ask the customer what he or she needs or wants, then show how this can be done with the use of your products and services – nothing more!

'I COULD HAVE SAID THAT'

During this section I have tried to emphasise the value of using the customer's words and expressions. To reinforce that, let me tell you about the time that I had a meeting to discuss sales training with a large firm of commercial property managers and estate agents. During the course of this meeting, the senior partner said, 'You have to understand that our people are professionals in the truest sense of the word, in that they are surveyors, valuers, etc., so the American hard-sell approach would be inappropriate.' As a result of taking copious notes during this meeting, I was able to present my proposal at the return meeting, part of which read 'Bearing in mind that your people are professionals in the truest sense of the word, we believe that an American style hard-sell approach would be singularly inappropriate. With this in mind we would recommend ...'

As the Senior Partner was reading this, he stopped and remarked, 'You know, Mr Cowden, you obviously understand our business. I could have said that myself.'

If he reads this book he will learn that he did!

CHECKLIST – CHAPTER 5

■ Your presentation should either solve problems or create opportunities.

■ Only make your presentation after you have summarised the customer's needs and desires and the customer is in agreement with your summary.

■ How to make the presentation: There are two aspects to your presentation, the verbal and the physical.

■ Don't forget the vocal part of the presentation: 'If you wish to be heard – speak softly!'

■ Remember the name of the game is 'empathy selling'

■ KISS

6

When the customer says no!

I have heard an expression in this business which says that the selling only begins the first time the customer says NO! I don't agree.

First of all, I believe that the selling begins with the very first contact that you have with the customer whether this is on the telephone or 'face-to-face'.

Secondly, I really do think that this type of thinking takes us back to the projection selling 'tennis match' between the customer and the sales person referred to in the last chapter.

There are a number of reasons why the customer says NO! among which are the following:

1   You haven't correctly identified the needs or desires.

2   You haven't adequately outlined the features and benefits.

3   The customer needs more information to make a YES decision.

4   The customer tells you lies!

The answers to questions 1, 2 and 3 are self-explanatory in the techniques being given to you in this book.

THE CUSTOMER TELLS YOU LIES!

There may be some customers who tell the most outrageous big black lies but they are in the minority. John Winkler, in his book *Pricing for Results* says, 'Buyers can be real miseries when they try hard, their mothers should have kissed them more.' Sometimes you simply come across one of these!

The majority of customers do, however, tell little white lies – rather than say YES!

Why?

1   The person you're dealing with may not have the decision making authority – but they certainly won't tell you. If you think that this is the case, you need to qualify the decision-making process – and quick. I will be giving you some more information on how to do this in a later chapter.

2   It may simply be pure resistance to buy.

3   Perhaps the customer doesn't like you. Customers are uncomfortable about doing business with people they don't like.

4   Perhaps there is a 'hidden agenda'. This may very well fall within the emotional category 3 that I mentioned in Chapter 1 and could be associated with the personal relationship they have with, or loyalty they feel towards, the current supplier. It could even involve 'bribery and corruption' – but that would be unusual.

Irrespective of whether the lies are big ones or little ones, you will soon be able to spot them because as reasons for saying NO, they will be totally illogical. Whether the customer tell you lies or whether he or she makes excuses, whenever the customer says NO we call these objections.

So let's look at handling objections.

Handling objections

The first point I would like to make is that there are only two objections you have to fear:

1   The one you didn't hear – because it wasn't said.

2   The one you can't handle – albeit only at the moment.

Number 1 usually falls within the 'hidden agenda' category outlined in 4 above. Number 2 would usually be for one of the following three reasons:

1 Your product knowledge isn't good enough. If this is the case the answer is obvious: improve your product knowledge, short-term by asking colleagues and managers, long-term by getting into some serious study about what it is you are selling.

   Because I'm in the sales training business many people expect me to emphasise this aspect of a sales person's knowledge and skill. That isn't my position at all. You cannot ever sell anything that you don't understand. So if you are reading this book and think that without the highest degree of product knowledge it will be able to make you better at what you do, you are wrong. Know your product!

2 Your own company's current policy is in conflict with what the customer wants. If this is the case you need to ask yourself if your company policy is wrong, but you will find that this isn't usually the case. Companies arrive at policy decisions for very good reasons. Perhaps you need to ask questions to understand what the policy is and why.

   I remember working with a major timber company and at this point in the programme one of their sales people told me that his biggest problem was that the accounts department kept putting his customers on hold – because they had exceeded their credit limit, with the result that he wasn't able to sell them any more until they had paid their bills. That was the company policy. My reply was that until the customer had paid the bills he hadn't sold anything at all – the customer had borrowed it! It's easy to 'sell' something to someone who doesn't pay for it.

3 There is a management problem within your own organisation. This is unfortunately more common than many people would expect. Until the management problem is resolved there is nothing you can do about it. If the problem isn't resolved eventually you need to reconsider your position and join another company where the problem doesn't exist. However, make sure that it is a management problem and it isn't just excuses you are making for failing to sell!

75

We will now consider the objections we can handle, but before we do I would like to ask you: What is a sales person's usual reaction to objections?

I'm not particularly fond of cartoons in books like this, but I have to include the following one that I use on training programmes, because it is so accurate in terms of how a customer sees you when he has thrown you the famous 'wobbler'!

I know some customers who do it deliberately just to see this reaction.

76

PANIC!!

Fig 6.1 Panic!!

To make sure that your reaction is not what the customer gleefully expects, the following technique will help.

After you have summarised, made your presentation and asked for the order – and the customer 'hits' you with the objection, PAUSE.

Remember the power of silence; the customer may continue talking giving you more details of the 'problem'. By pausing you give the customer time to think. The pause gives you time to think. If you pause and look thoughtful (body language) at the same time, the customer will think that you are giving careful consideration to what he or she has said.

The pause allows you to collect yourself so that even if you panic it doesn't show.

TELL ME MORE! The three magic words again. Get the customer to continue talking so that you obtain more information about the reason why he or she isn't ready to buy – YET! The customer may get something 'off the chest' and feel better for it. The customer might begin to supply the answer to the objection. You gain yourself even more thinking time.

'APART FROM THAT...?' Make sure that you get out all of the objections so that you don't become involved in the infamous 'tennis match': Objection – Answer – New Objection – Answer – New Objection – Answer – New Objection – Answer, etc.

Go through this process and you could die of old age before you make a decent sale!

Ask the question:

'Apart from that is there anything else that would prevent you from doing business with us?' If you get a 'Yes!' answer you need to go back into 'Digging for Gold' to discover the problem that escaped your attention before. If you get a 'No!' answer you can continue with – 'IF I CAN SATISFY YOU REGARDING THAT...?' You are now about to make sure that the customer can't come back to you with any more daft excuses.

'If I can satisfy you regarding that situation can we talk serious business?' You've not only made sure that the 'tennis match' is over, you have gone for some real commitment from the customer.

PRESENT YOUR ANSWER. Now handle the objection in the very best way that you can and **ask**: 'ARE YOU SATISFIED WITH THAT?'

If you have handled the objection well the customer will have no alternative to saying 'Yes' and you will now ask for the order – won't you!

If the customer isn't satisfied, you either weren't able to handle the objection properly or the customer is playing games. You will know based on the things that were outlined earlier in this chapter if the customer should be satisfied with the answer and will therefore know if he or she is 'games playing' or maybe there's a 'hidden agenda'.

I wonder, however, how many times you have left the customer's premises having failed to handle all of the objections and get the business, when, as you're driving to the next call, the thought occurs to you, 'I wish I had remembered to say...'. The problem is that in the heat of the moment we forget some of the previous situations where we handled similar objections highly successfully. To help you overcome these 'memory losses' we will now create an **Objection File**.

The objection file

I use the document we are about to create in much the same way that I file information that comes into my office. Whenever I receive something new I file it away for future reference and retrieve it when it is needed. We will do exactly the same with the **Objection File**.

Using the following form, list the most common objections you encounter – with the exception of price objections – and the best possible answer you have devised to handle these;

Having completed that exercise I should explain that I asked you to exclude price because it is such a special subject that the next chapter is devoted to it in its entirety.

Having created your objection file, make sure that whenever you go into a call you have it to hand so that you can minimise the 'I wish I had said that...' occasions.

The final part of this chapter deals with the best way of handling objections I have come across, when it can be done.

Pre-handling objections

INCLUDING 'DISCLOSURE'

From the objection file you have created try to identify those that are sufficiently common that you can pre-handle them. All I mean by this is that **you** raise the objections during your conversation and handle them so that they don't come back later.

79

Think of some of the common objections in your business, for example:

- Service
- Reliability
- Availability
- Continuity of supply
- Quality of materials
- Validity of guarantees, etc.

Then bring these into your conversation showing how your company deals with each of these. Every objection you can get out and handle as part of your 'sale' before you ask for the order is one less that is lurking to attack you when you least expect it. It makes the completion of the sale a lot easier and in fact makes it a logical conclusion to your conversation with the customer.

Make a list of the most common objections you hear and the best answers you have been able to use to handle them.

1-Obj.	
1-Ans.	
2-Obj.	
2-Ans.	
3-Obj.	
3-Ans.	
4-Obj.	
4-Ans.	
5-Obj.	
5-Ans.	
6-Obj.	
6-Ans.	
7-Obj.	
7-Ans.	
8-Obj.	
8-Ans.	
9-Obj.	
9-Ans.	
10-Obj.	
10-Ans.	

Fig 6.2 Objections

Disclosure is similar but goes a stage further.

My good friend Derek Stables, the retired director of management education and training for Ciba Geigy plc, used to refer to this as 'If all else fails try honesty', but he was only joking (I think). It actually goes beyond that and makes honesty the pre-requisite.

Early in your conversation, raise the type of genuine fears that you know buyers have in your business. Check that these are the types of things that may concern this customer and then show how the fears are groundless when doing business with your company.

The example from the training business would be that many customers worry about whether or not the training will work. I would then ask if that is the type of concern that this customer could have. When I get the affirmative reply I am able to explain that my company puts in place a system of agreed measurement criteria which shows the performance of the people before the training and then continually measures it, against the same criteria, on a monthly basis thereafter, allowing the customer to measure and show the improvement.

81

Whether you are in insurance, car sales, office equipment, engineering or any other business, there will be classics in your business that lend themselves to this type of objection pre-handling. Use them!

THE NEXT TIME I SAW IT, IT WAS IN PRINT!

I had a discussion about 'disclosure' with Rod Leaver who was then the sales director of Commercial Union Financial Services based in Croydon, but who is now Managing Director of Laurentian Financial Advisers in Gloucester.

I had worked with Rod when he initially set up the direct sales force for CUFS and have been constantly impressed by his professionalism, integrity, down-to-earth approach and fairness. The fact that he is also one of the most likeable and humorous people you would ever wish to meet is an absolute bonus.

During our discussion about 'disclosure' we discussed some of the 'infamous' practices in the life insurance industry, which the financial services legislation was being brought into being to eradicate or at least minimise:

1   Pressurising people to sign on the night, usually with the 'fear' close; the one that suggests that if you die before you sign the application your family will not be adequately protected – so you had better sign it now!

2   Recommending policies on the basis of what the sales person would earn, rather than their suitability to the customer's needs.

3   Exaggerated claims of performance and projections of future values.

As Rod and his managing director at CUFS were among the forerunners in making sure that the sales force didn't become involved in these practices I suggested that he should take advantage of that, highlight these points to customers and then point out that none of these applied to CUFS, including signing on the night.

By doing this I believed that he would increase the credibility of his sales force and his company and in the long term it would pay dividends. Some six weeks later I was sitting in reception at Rod Leaver's offices waiting to meet him when I picked up the company newsletter to read while I waited, and there was our discussion in print, almost verbatim.

Obviously the idea was a good one and I was pleased that he thought enough of it to tell his sales people.

THE HOLIDAY INN, GLASGOW

My final story about 'disclosure' relates to its use in an entirely different context.

There will be times when you make an absolute mess of something, perhaps during your presentation. I have found that when this happens the customer knows – so own up. The credibility you will gain by being honest and human is immeasurable. The best opportunity I ever had to practice this was in the late 1980s.

The government-sponsored Scottish Development Agency was holding an open-day seminar on marketing for small businesses at The Holiday Inn in Glasgow and I had been invited to give a talk on sales and selling.

I managed to arrange it so that I was the last speaker of the day and found out that the person immediately preceding me, who by coincidence was also a friend of mine, was talking about marketing. I arranged to sit through his speech in order to take some notes and create links between his talk and mine so as to add value to both presentations.

The time came for me to go on stage where I would make my presentation with the aid of an overhead projector and my pre-prepared presentation acetates. There were a couple of hundred people present and the room was in semi-darkness to make the screen easier to see.

About halfway through my presentation I broke one of the golden rules about using overhead projectors, which is never point to the screen, it means that you turn your back to the audience. You should always point towards the acetate on the projector itself where you remain facing the audience and can still see everything that they can.

In my enthusiasm to reinforce a point I walked to the back of the stage to point to the screen whereupon I discovered that the stage didn't go as far back as the wall holding the screen – and promptly disappeared, having fallen off. The audience totally collapsed in fits of laughter – and I still had half of my presentation to make.

I climbed back on stage and walked to the front of it. When the room had quietened sufficiently for me to be heard, I said,

'Ladies and gentlemen, I have been making this type of presentation for some years now but before I came on stage this afternoon I still felt nervous. Would anybody like to guess how I'm feeling now?' At which point, in typical Glasgow humour, a voice from the back of the room called out, 'It's OK Jim, somebody fell down there this morning, but we didn't want him to get back up again!'

The 'disclosure' saved the day, the presentation continued and was extremely successful, so much so that for some time there was a degree of debate about whether I had fallen off deliberately as an attention grabber. I can assure you that I hadn't, but there are still some people in Scotland who remember me as the man who fell off the stage at the Holiday Inn!

CHECKLIST – CHAPTER 6

■ Understand why you get objections.

■ Remember that customers will sometimes tell you lies rather than simply say NO!

■ Beware the 'hidden agenda'.

■ Practice the technique for handling the objections and make it work for you.

■ Create your own objection file and use it – and keep it updated.

■ Pre-handle the most common objections.

■ Use 'disclosure' – and use it to your advantage.

85

Talking about price

Why are we afraid of talking price?

We have been told so often that price is the totally overriding factor that we have come to believe it.

IT'S NOT TRUE!

If it was true, no one would ever buy a Rolex watch, a Rolls Royce car, a Mercedes-Benz or a cashmere sweater. In fact, in these examples, most of these have made price one of their selling features.

87

I remember a conversation I had in Marbella in Spain with a dealer who specialised in one of the most expensive watches in the world. I asked him how the watch business was doing, whereupon he replied, 'I haven't a clue, nobody ever bought one of my watches to be able to tell the time. I'm not in the watch business. I'm in the status business!'

I still have a copy of a magazine advertisement for perfume which says, 'Joy & "1000" the costliest perfumes in the world... Jean Patou, Paris'.

However, I'm sure that most of you reading this book are saying to yourselves, 'That's all very well, but I'm not in the status business, I'm in Agriculture or Pharmaceuticals or Domestic Appliances or whatever.' I simply want to get the message across that we have become conditioned to thinking price is the 'be-all-and end-all' of our customers' buying criteria.

Let me come a little closer to home – my own business of training.

In the area of training where I work, price would never be a serious consideration when choosing between using me or using one of my competitors. The bottom line would be who can deliver the best training. Once that had been decided, price would become one of the negotiating variables, but it wouldn't be the number one consideration.

If there are any 'unprofessional' buyers of training who have managed to get their hands on this book, I hope you are taking note!

So if we have been conditioned to believing that price is what it is ALL about, who has been responsible for this?

1 Unprofessional sales people who use this as the most common excuse for not winning orders.

2 Customers who have played this game so successfully that they have won by virtue of the fact that we do believe it.

Another reason why we hate talking price, unless of course we are at the bottom end of the market selling the 'cheap and nastys' where price is our only selling feature, is that it is the final opportunity the customer has to raise an objection – just when we thought things were going so well!

So try to get **some clearer thinking** about price.

Remember that price is often the only weapon that the customer has, and the way to disarm this argument is to convince the customer that you are there to solve problems or create opportunities – not to get involved in a fight. Be aware of the fact that we so often hear that we are too expensive that we start to believe it ourselves. The only answer to this dilemma is to examine your pricing, understand it and that way you will believe in your own pricing structure. You will always lose orders because of price – there will always be someone desperate enough to undercut you – but also remember that the cheapest doesn't necessarily sell.

You will never consistently be the cheapest – even at the bottom end of the market – but customers don't only buy at a price, they buy on a value for money relationship. At the end of the day you need to realise that handling price goes with the territory – it's part of the job!

That being the case, let us now look at some of the words we use.

The words we use

The words we use to describe our 'price' create distinct impressions in the minds of our customers – even if only subconsciously. We will begin with the worst that I have come across and gradually develop towards the best.

1 The Damage

This is the most negative expression I have ever come across. It is the language of the shady used cars dealer and others of that ilk and is usually accompanied by some form of address like, 'Chief' or 'Squire' or 'Matey'.

89

2 Cost

This is another highly negative expression although not nearly as bad as 'damage'. It implies an outlay with no return.

3 Price or Charge or Rate

Other negative expressions suggesting an outlay with no return, although in talking to customers they do at least prefer these to 'cost'.

4 At or For

Either of these is a fairly neutral expression which doesn't conjure up thoughts of 'cost'.

5 Fee

A good positive word this, mainly because it suggests professionalism. It may not be that there is any suggestion of a return but the professional nature of the word implies specialisation and value for money.

6 Investment

The only expression here where a return is implicit in the use of the word. By far and away the most positive of them all.

What you need to do is think about your business and the words that are most appropriate – by checking them through in the reverse order in which they have been written here so that you try to select the most positive word that you can to describe your 'price'.

If the customer can genuinely expect a return from the product or service that you have to offer, use the word **investment**. Remember that the return doesn't have to be measured in monetary terms. In the training business it is now so accepted that there is a return on the investment of time, money and resources that this word is highly appropriate.

The word **fee** may very well apply most appropriately in the professions but its usage is now becoming acceptable in many specialised and service industries.

Carry on through the list yourself and arrive at the best word for you – then use it.

Making the price presentation

The first thing to remember is try not to present your price until after the customer has accepted your summary of the needs and desires and understands the benefits which will accrue from buying your product or service.

You may not always succeed in this but we will come back to ways of trying to do so when we look at the early price challenge.

Once the customer knows what he or she is getting for the price it is possible for them to make a value for money judgement. Until then you will have fallen into the buyers' price trap – again.

90

When you have succeeded in getting the customer to realise the benefits you should be able to link the 'price' to the benefits thereby reducing the impact of the price.

For example, 'Mrs Smith, your investment of £50 per month in our cellular telephone system will give you the round-the-clock contact with your service engineers that you said was so important to you in looking after your customers.'

Here is an even better example: 'In order to improve the ability of your sales people to win business and get results, your investment of £5000 will also give you a system of monitoring and measuring their improvement on an on-going basis.'

What makes this example better is that I have been able to put a different benefit on either side of the price. It reduces the impact of the price by hiding it and introduces additional benefits, increasing the value for money thinking. In your business it may not always be possible to do that, but you must at least link your price to one benefit. If you can't think quickly enough to do this when you are face-to-face, remember to do it when writing to your customer confirming the details of your offer.

You will always get customers, however, who will try to convince you that price is the only consideration and therefore they want you to cut out all of the sales talk and tell them what the price is. It is called the 'early price challenge'.

The early price challenge

You must have been in the situation where, during your presentation, the customer threw in a remark along the lines of, 'I'll bet that's **expensive**?' Don't fall into the trap, **ignore it**!

If this is a genuine concern about the price it will come back later in your conversation as a real question, 'How much will it cost?' Interestingly you will note that customers don't use positive words like investment or fee, they use the most negative words they can find to apply to the situation. I have

91

even had some very high-profile customers ask me, 'What's the Damage?' If you are asked for the price try to get your benefits message across first. Use delaying expressions like:

1   I'm just coming to that.

2   That will depend on exactly what you want.

3   Let me tell you what you will be getting first. Then carry on without giving the price.

4   I'll leave you with full price details at the end.

If the customer is persistently interrupting you about the price, go on the attack and try to get some commitment with expressions like:

1   Is price your only consideration?

2   Price is obviously important to you, so if the price is right will you give me the business? That one usually shuts them up!

3   What size of order did you want to place? Ouch!

4   Are you ready to place an order then?

If you are really being pressed before you can get all of the benefits out, the chances are that the customer is 'playing the game', so give a 'ball park' figure and carry on without waiting for a reaction, something along the lines of, 'It'll be in the £300 region but as I was saying, what you will get is...'

If we work on the principle that you have managed to make a decent presentation and you have then given the price in the way that I suggested, don't be surprised if the customer doesn't rush out to get you a purchase order! There is another little hurdle waiting for you; it's called the price objection!

Handling the price objection

There are two basic types of price objection;

1   The price is more than the customer can afford.

2   The one where the customer didn't expect the price to be as high, either based on lack of knowledge or based on a competitive price.

Let's look at both.

THE ONE THAT THE CUSTOMER CAN'T AFFORD

In this situation I would have to place the blame for this on the sales person's shoulders because this type of information should have been uncovered in 'Digging for Gold'. So the chances are that it's your fault. However, if you find yourself in this situation you need to reconsider your offer. Do you have a less expensive alternative that would suit the customer's needs? Can you reduce the technical specification to bring the price within the customer's reach? Have you just been wasting each other's time?

THE ONE THAT APPEARS TOO HIGH COMPARED TO THE CUSTOMER'S EXPECTATIONS OR A COMPETITIVE OFFER

This one used to be relatively easy to spot because the customer would use the word 'expensive' in the proper context, that is, in comparison to something else. Nowadays the word is misused and we have to double check to clarify the situation.

When you hear the objection, 'expensive', ask, 'compared to what?' If you get a reply along the lines of, 'Compared to what I can afford to pay', you know that you're back in the realms of the previous situation and have to reconsider your offer. If, as is more likely, you get a reply along the lines of, 'Compared to what I'm paying at the moment', you know that it could be a real objection and you now have to handle it.

You now have to find out what you're up against in terms of price. Ask the customer, 'How much money are we talking about?' A lot of sales people try to tell me that the customer won't tell you the price that you're up against. This may be true at the beginning of your meeting but not after you've

93

presented your price. In fact, they not only give you an indication of the price that you're up against, they **'massage'** it!. That's one of my little euphemisms for 'telling lies'.

If the customer is expecting to pay or currently paying £300, you are likely to be told something like £280 – or even less. If your knowledge of your products, your market place, your competitors and your pricing structure is what it ought to be, you will spot the 'massage' immediately.

I was in a call with a customer's sales manager recently where he was trying to win an order to supply timber pallets. As soon as the customer supplied the price, he knew that it had to be for second-hand pallets, whereas he was selling new ones. The customer wasn't making a 'like-for-like' comparison. The answers in that situation were either to compete by offering second-hand pallets or sell the benefits of new ones against second-hand. In any event it was obvious what had to be done.

Whether the customer is telling little lies or not – and it is all part of the game – what you now have to do is **restate the difference in price, minimising it if possible**. **To minimise the difference you have two alternatives**: use the straight cash figure or convert it to a percentage difference, whichever sounds less. If the customer tells you that the difference is £200 and that represents a difference of two per cent, say, 'So we are talking about a difference of two per cent?' If the customer has said that the price difference is seven per cent and that represents a cash difference of forty pence, say, 'So we are talking about a difference of forty pence?'

You now have to do a direct comparison between your product and the competition. Get the customer to tell you exactly what he or she gets for the current price: quality, delivery, after sales guarantee, etc., so that you know what you have extra to offer. As soon as you have this information – believe me the customer will give it to you – you have to sell the difference!

If necessary do it on a piece of paper with the customer, although I have always been more comfortable with doing this verbally. Go through all of the **features** that the customer is currently getting for the price, 'ticking off' those that he or she will also get with your product. When you have exhausted the list you will have the additional ones which you have to offer. Leave the competitor's features as features but convert your additional features into benefits and sell these to the customer for the difference in price. You don't have to sell the whole price, your competitor had already sold most of that before you arrived. You only need to **sell the difference!**

There will be occasions when the competitor has more features than you, simply different ones. By leaving the competitor's features as features, you will minimise the customer's perception of their value.

The practice outlined above is quite common these days in the world of advertising, particularly with motor cars. I'm sure you have seen the press advertisements where there is a table containing a column of features with a comparison between two or more motor cars and a tick list which shows which car has most features. Invariably, by careful selection of the features, the motor manufacturer who has paid for the advertisement turns out to provide the car with most features.

My personal belief is that a wonderful opportunity has been missed, certainly in all of the advertisements that I have seen, to convert the additional features into benefits.

Some of the features that I see being promoted over the competition are:

- ABS (Anti-lock Braking System) – Yes?

I think it should read something like: A B S – the additional safety feature which allows you to brake suddenly while still maintaining control of the vehicle.

- SIPS (Side Impact Intrusion System) – OK?

SIPS – the additional safety feature which gives both driver and passengers extra protection in the event of a collision from the side.

■ Electrically heated front windscreen – Yawn!

Electrically heated front windscreen – the additional safety feature that ensures clear vision at all times for the driver.

There are more but I hope you get my point. Think about this when you are involved in selling your products in a competition situation.

Even after you have successfully handled the price objection there will be customers who will want to do a little price bargaining. The most important thing about this stage in the sale is that, with very few exceptions, you have already won the order – the customer is just looking for a little extra. Customers don't waste time bargaining with people who aren't going to get the business.

Compromise: If the customer wants a better price – give it, providing you get a better order! That way you will both be happy with the outcome.

The effect of discounting

Whatever you do, don't get locked into the discounting game out of desperation. All that will happen is that the customer will recognise this and play all of the competitors off against each other until somebody cracks.

I have reproduced here two tables, one which shows the extra business that you need to win to maintain the same level of profitability, whenever you offer discounts, the other showing the amount of business you can afford to lose and still maintain your profitability whenever you increase your prices. These figures are based on the gross profit margin in your company so you may have to ask your boss about these figures. (*N.B.*: contribution is gross profit.)

Price Discount in %	Gross profit margin %							
	25.0	30.0	35.0	40.0	45.0	50.0	55.0	60.0
	% Volume turnover required to give unchanged contribution							
2.5	111.1	109.1	107.7	106.7	105.9	105.3	104.8	104.3
5.0	125.0	120.0	116.7	114.3	112.5	111.1	110.0	109.1
7.5	142.9	133.3	127.3	123.1	120.0	117.6	115.8	114.3
10.0	166.7	150.0	140.0	133.3	128.6	125.0	122.2	120.0
12.5	200.0	171.4	155.6	145.5	138.5	133.3	129.4	126.3
15.0	250.0	200.0	175.0	160.0	150.0	142.9	137.5	133.3
17.5	333.3	240.0	200.0	177.8	163.6	153.8	146.7	141.2
20.0	500.0	300.0	233.3	200.0	180.0	166.7	157.1	150.0
22.5	1000.0	400.0	280.0	228.6	200.0	181.8	169.2	160.0
25.0		600.0	350.0	266.7	225.0	200.0	183.3	171.4

Fig 7.1 The effect of discounting

Price Discount in %	Gross profit margin %							
	25.0	30.0	35.0	40.0	45.0	50.0	55.0	60.0
	% Volume turnover required to give unchanged contribution							
2.5	90.9	92.3	93.3	94.1	94.7	95.2	95.7	96.0
5.0	83.3	85.7	87.5	88.9	90.0	90.9	91.7	92.3
7.5	76.9	80.0	82.4	84.2	85.7	87.0	88.0	88.9
10.0	71.4	75.0	77.8	80.0	81.8	83.3	84.6	85.7
12.5	66.7	70.6	73.7	76.2	78.3	80.0	81.5	82.8
150	62.5	66.7	70.0	72.7	75.0	76.9	78.6	80.0
17.5	58.8	63.2	66.7	69.6	72.0	74.1	75.9	77.4
20.0	55.6	60.0	63.6	66.7	69.2	71.4	73.3	75.0
22.5	52.6	57.1	60.9	64.0	66.7	69.0	71.0	72.7
25.0	50.0	54.5	58.3	61.5	64.3	66.7	68.8	70.6

Fig 7.2 The effect of price increases

£1000 TO CLEAN A FLOOR!

When I worked with Exclusive Contract Cleaning in Scotland I received a call one day from a club on the outskirts of Glasgow that had recently suffered from a fire in the kitchen. As a result of this there was considerable smoke damage to the floor of the dance room area. The call was to ask for a quotation to clean this smoke damaged floor and restore it to the proper condition.

I had only been with the company for about three weeks at which point my in-depth knowledge of what would be involved to carry out this exercise was about as good as my expertise in brain surgery! I duly visited the club, spoke with the people concerned about what they needed the end result to be and took notes so that I could discuss this with people in the company who did know what would be involved.

It was going to be a delicate operation and after some discussion I asked one of the cleaning supervisors to visit the site with me to make sure that we presented a good case for winning the contract, as I knew we would be up against some pretty stiff competition. As she surveyed the damaged area I got her to tell me what exactly she would do and why.

I returned to the office and with the aid of the managing director we prepared a price for the contract onto which we added a significant safety and profit margin in case we ran into unforeseen problems. I wasn't able to pin the decision-maker down to an appointment so I submitted a two-page proposal in which I detailed every stage of the operation (the features of the service) and what the result of doing these things would be (the benefits). I followed up the proposal with several telephone calls to find out how successful we had been but was unable to close down a decision on the telephone or arrange a face-to-face meeting. Two weeks later I did get a telephone call from the decision-maker to ask when we could carry out the work as the proposal had been successful. During this call he also remarked, 'I have to tell you that your price was at least twice that of the nearest alternative tender, but we had to give you the contract as you were the only people who made us feel that you knew what you were doing!' After three weeks?

For those of you who perhaps haven't grasped the significance of the actual price, the equivalent in 1994 terms would be around the £4000 mark – just to clean a floor!

CHECKLIST – CHAPTER 7

■ Don't be afraid of talking about price.

■ Be careful about the words you use and select those which work best for you.

■ Wrap your benefits around the price to create a value for money perception

■ Recognise the early price challenge and delay it until the customer understands the benefits of what is on offer.

■ Practice handling the price objections and when in competition remember that you only need to sell the difference!

■ Bargain – give a better price for a better order.

■ Recognise the effect of discounting.

8

The beginning and the end

So far we have looked at much of what you need to do when you are face to face with your customers. In this chapter I would like to address the beginning of the process when you arrive at the customer's premises, after which I will move on to the point where you leave with an order in your pocket and a smile on your face!

Before I continue, however, I think that the reason you are reading this book probably falls into one of three categories:

1   You have been on one of my company's training programmes, in which case all of this is refresher and reinforcement for you.

2   You have deliberately sought out this book for your own development, because you want to be better.

3   Your manager has given you this book to 'buck you up'.

In the first two cases you know that you need to be better and different from all the rest of the sales people out there and in the third you have already come to terms with that or you wouldn't have read this far. So let's continue and see if we can indeed make you better and different from the 'run of the mill'.

Initial impressions

SELLING YOURSELF!

You will never get a second chance to create a good first impression!

IN RECEPTION

If you want to be taken seriously by receptionists, the majority of whom have developed cynicism to an art form, you need to:

- Be positive
- Look professional
- Maintain your dignity.

If you have an appointment, don't say things like, 'I have an appointment with Mrs Brown', or, 'Mrs Brown is expecting me'. **Be much more positive and say 'Mrs Brown asked me to call at...'** It's true. If you arranged an appointment for a mutually convenient time, then your customer asked you to call at a certain time. Use that approach and watch the change in the receptionist's attitude to you compared to all of the other 'peddlers' that walk through the door. I can assure you that 'peddlers' is how receptionists see you. Change that perception and create the impression that you are different, that you are not a peddler, you are a business person.

If you have no specific appointment you won't be able to use this approach so you will have to think of other ways of creating a professional impression. Don't say, 'I was in the area and "popped in" to see if Mrs Brown was available'. Say, 'Mrs Brown made a point of asking me to call to see her when I was in this area and could make the time. Is she available at the moment?' I'm assuming that when you last spoke to Mrs Brown she said something like, 'Its difficult to set an appointment, but you can call in when you're next in the area'. Basically a 'brush off' but one that you could try to turn to your advantage.

In these situations or if it's a straight cold call, there are other things that you will want to consider.

Ask yourself, 'Do I really need to carry this briefcase and all the other paraphernalia that makes me look more like a sample carrier than a serious business person?' If you have to carry a lot of material, can you leave the bulky stuff in the car until you have made contact with your 'buyer'? You may also want to consider the situation where you meet a really friendly receptionist and you are offered coffee or tea while you wait. The best message I can give you about that situation is in the following experience: I was doing some field accompaniment with the national account manager of a pharmaceutical company when we arrived in reception for a pre-arranged appointment. As is not unusual, we were not the only people waiting to be seen. Among the others was a fairly smart looking young man complete with briefcase and an A2 size portfolio carrier (obviously with some type of display material). The receptionist had been extremely considerate and organised a cup of coffee for him. Halfway through his coffee, his appointment arrived at reception to take him through to a private office for his meeting, whereupon he stood up, collected his briefcase in one hand, his A2 Portfolio in the other and proceeded to try to carry his coffee cup through to the meeting without spilling the contents all over the floor. It was one of the most comical juggling acts I have seen outside of a circus! It took me all of my restraint not to collapse in fits of laughter. Extremely entertaining for me, but the poor man had destroyed any illusions of dignity or professionalism.

103

For heaven's sake, leave the coffee behind!

At the same appointment, my colleague from the pharmaceutical company had taken his briefcase into the customer's offices and while we were waiting I asked him if he really needed to carry it. His reply was that he had always carried a briefcase into appointments. That was all right by me, but when we went into our meeting I made a point of noting when he used it. Halfway through our meeting he opened his briefcase, took out an A4 size diary and from inside this he took out two single sheets of A4 paper containing some figures that he had promised to get for his customer. That was all.

When we were driving to the next call I spoke to him about this and asked him why he hadn't simply taken in the diary.

At the next appointment, to humour me, he worked out what he needed to take into the call and this time he only took in his diary, inside of which he placed a brochure. When our meeting was over, everything had gone well although he hadn't even needed to use the brochure.

We again spoke in the car on our way to the next appointment and I asked him how he had felt about not having the briefcase. He said that at first it had felt a little strange after years of automatically having it with him but that as the meeting progressed he realised that he had more physical freedom, not having to worry about where to put his briefcase or how to open it without causing disruption, and that he thought the customer appeared a lot more relaxed than usual – despite the fact that there were two of us visiting him.

104

Now I know that for some of you, the briefcase and some of the other accoutrements are necessary, but not always. The problem with the briefcase is that many customers see it as some kind of loaded gun and worry that you will dive into it and take out something that they have to sign. If you don't need the briefcase for any other reason, lull them into a false sense of security; carry the order form inside the back of a reasonably-sized diary and let the customer relax. You will still be prepared for when you have to close the sale.

Some of the stuff I have seen sales people take into customer's premises, often unnecessarily, has been so bulky, you would think that they had reversed the car up to reception and emptied the contents of the boot. If you want to be treated like a serious business person, look like a serious business person.

I have tried to give you some pointers regarding being positive, looking professional and maintaining your dignity and I would like to share one other experience with you that I had recently in a customer's reception area.

I had an appointment with the managing director of a large packaging company in north London. While I waited to be seen, another sales person came into reception and having spoken to the receptionist, sat down to wait to be called. A couple of minutes later there was a distinctive sound from his briefcase whereupon he opened it, retrieved his portable telephone and conducted a conversation in the middle of reception. Notwithstanding the fact that it was downright unprofessional – he should have switched the damn thing off – he didn't know who I was! I could have been a competitor of his company, in which case the information I was able to overhear from his conversation would have been extremely helpful to me in future sales against him!

IN FRONT OF THE CUSTOMER

It takes ninety seconds to form a first impression:

105

- Thirty eight per cent is based on **how we speak**
- Seven per cent is based on **what we actually say**
- Fifty-five per cent is based on **how we look**.

Obviously the major factors here are how we speak and how we look and I will be expanding on these before we leave this chapter.

To maximise on the impression that you give your customer;

Remember the three 'Twelves':

1 The first twelve inches, that is, your face. Look confident and friendly. Smile!

2 The first twelve steps. Walk towards the customer in an upright, positive and confident manner. Don't shuffle or slouch.

3 The first twelve words. Make sure that your personal greeting is full of confidence and enthusiasm and that it makes the customer feel pleased to meet you.

Whenever you have an appointment, remember the following:

be on time!

If you made an appointment in the first place it was because both you and the customer are busy people. It therefore becomes the most appalling bad manners to turn up late as if you didn't value the customer's time – or your own.

be smart

Don't insult the customer by turning up as if you were about to dig the garden or go hill walking.

be planned

Have all the various features and benefits analyses, etc. with you. Make sure that you also have your objection file. Being planned is highly professional and buyers can spot the difference between professional sales people and unprofessional sales people immediately.

When you begin your conversation with the customer, **get to the point as soon as possible**. The number of sales people who 'waffle' for what seems an eternity when they find themselves in front of customers is an insult to the profession. You are supposed to be busy people doing business with equally busy, or even busier, people. So stop messing about talking about the weather, cricket, fashion, football, etc. Get to the point!

There are some organisations with whom I have worked who even encourage this 'waffle' by talking about things like 'scene setting'. It may very well have some validity but at the end of the day it tends to encourage sales people to delay getting to the point of the call – talking about business!

I also understand that if you know the customer there is some time for social chit-chat that will help to improve the relationship between you, but don't be afraid to get down to business – it's why you're there. Do the selling first and leave the pleasantries and social chit-chat to the end!

State the purpose of your call!

Busy buyers see many people during the course of a day. Even if you set up the meeting with an appointment, the buyer has probably forgotten why you are there. Remind the buyer.

Get the customer to want to answer your questions!

Remember 'Digging for Gold'.

Be firm and positive!

Behave in this manner and you increase the probability of being dealt with professionally and with respect. Don't do it and you run the risk that the buyer will walk all over you.

Be enthusiastic!

107

If you can't be enthusiastic about the products or services that you sell, why should you expect the customer to become so. The wonderful thing about enthusiasm is that it is so infectious. If you display enthusiasm about what you are selling the customer will become enthusiastic too!

Enthusiasm is so vital, not only in selling but in everything that you want to do well that I would like to expand on it just a little.

Show me the top sales people in your company or the top sales branch or team and I promise you that the one thing they have in common is enthusiasm for what they do. Show me Boy Scouts or Girl Guides who are the top fundraisers for their organisations and you will find people with enthusiasm. Show me anyone who has reached the top of their profession and I'll show you people with enthusiasm for what they do and how well they do it. Enthusiasm, excellence and success are all totally interlinked.

In the final chapter of this book I will give you a plan for success, which will include modelling yourself on successful people. I think it's appropriate here to give you just one example of such a person in the context of enthusiasm.

While running the SmithKline Beecham 'Graduate Overview Programme', I had the pleasure of meeting Peter Jensen (pronounced 'Yensen') who was then the top man in the UK for SmithKline Beecham Consumer Brands. Part of the programme which was run for the graduates involved the use of guest speakers from various parts of the company to make presentations on different aspects of the business with a view to giving the participants on the programme a broader understanding of the whole corporation. Peter's commitment and enthusiasm for this was such that whenever possible he made the presentation personally. His whole demeanour, his entire approach and the zest that he injected into this part of the programme was such that he was invariably rated as the top speaker when he was present – and this was from a group who were predominantly in research and development and who until then were not particularly interested in things like marketing, that was for people involved in the 'unsavoury' world of commercialism as opposed to the rarefied atmosphere of the laboratory!

If you check your bathroom cabinet or your kitchen cupboards you will find something there that 'belongs' to Peter Jensen. Aquafresh™ Toothpaste, Ribena™ fruit drinks, Lucozade™ drinks, Brylcreem™ grooming products, Horlicks™ drinks, etc.; the list is almost endless. Peter is as enthusiastic about his toothpaste as he is about his drinks and his hair care products and indeed the entire range. He is also as enthusiastic about the advertisements that promote them, many of them so well known that your recognition would be immediate. But it doesn't end there, Peter is also enthusiastic about the sales figures, the budgets and targets achieved, the market penetration, the market share, the sales growth year on year – in fact every aspect of his business.

Peter Jensen is, at the time of writing, the Chairman and Senior Vice President of SmithKline Beecham Consumer Health Care in Europe – yes, among the top in his profession. For anybody who has anything to do with marketing, sales, public speaking, management or excellence in anything, Peter should be a mandatory role model.

(Aquafresh, Ribena, Lucozade, Brylcreem and Horlicks are all, at the time of my experience and writing, trademarks of SmithKline Beecham Consumer Health Care, part of the transnational SmithKline Beecham Corporation.)

Be polite!

For reasons which escape me, people have become used to accepting the most awful standards of behaviour in business from colleagues, customers and suppliers: rudeness from people who can't differentiate between assertiveness and aggression; arrogance from people who confuse this with being positive; bullying from people who think this displays strength when in fact it is the opposite – and invariably comes from people who are weak and 'wimpish' in their domestic or social lives. There are many more examples too numerous to include here.

109

In fact many of the standards of behaviour we accept would be such that if displayed by our children would earn them the firmest of rebukes. So be polite, your customer will find it extremely refreshing.

Make notes

The average brain is capable of more than the most powerful computer but, as a notepad, even the best of brains usually comes a very poor second to pen and paper. Cast your mind back to 'Digging for Gold' and remember that to make use of all of the 'nuggets' you first need to remember them, so make sure that you write them down. Check with your customer first of all that this is all right, in case you are being exposed to confidential or sensitive information.

I would like to give you a further point for when you find yourself in front of the customer – in reception. There will be occasions when the customer keeps you in reception, even when you have an appointment. This is no way to conduct business. When this happens to you it is likely that the customer really doesn't want to have the meeting and is keeping you there so that the meeting will be short. It could also be that the customer knows that you will not be totally comfortable in reception and has kept you there as a tactic in order that he or she can have the upper hand. The first thing you must do is ask, 'Is there somewhere private where we can talk?' If it has been a simple matter of oversight on the customer's part, this will immediately be arranged; if not it means that either the customer doesn't really want to see you or it is a tactical move to make you uneasy. Seize the initiative! Tell the customer that there may be things that you would want to discuss that it may not be appropriate to do in a totally public area. If that doesn't work go for the shock tactics; ask sensitive questions!

I remember being in such a situation with an optician who wanted the meeting and presentation conducted in the reception area while there were patients waiting to be seen. I asked three simple questions:

1 What price do you normally pay for your soft contact lenses?

2 At what price would you normally sell them?

3 What would be the ideal profit figure you would hope to achieve on a pair of contact lenses?

Would you believe that a private meeting room suddenly became available with such speed that the optician could have easily been mistaken for a magician?

The moral of this story is that if you can't have the privacy you will never be able to keep the initiative and you may as well run the risk of terminating the meeting until a more suitable time. You are never going to do real business in this environment anyway, so kill the situation stone dead! The next time you have an appointment with such a person it will be conducted in a professional manner. Sales people say to me, 'But I might never get another appointment if I do that.'

That's fine by me. You weren't going to get any business anyway, so you may as well take your activity somewhere else where it's more appreciated and more effective. The one thing I know for sure is that if you do get an appointment with that customer in the future, you will be taken seriously.

Let's return to the subject of punctuality. I know that I tell you to be on time, but any of you who have to work in major cities like London, Paris, Rome or New York will know that even if you have managed to fight your way through the traffic to arrive at your destination on time, you then have to find a parking place! It's easy to say that you should make allowance for this when you plan your calls, but hold-ups do happen. I had to conduct a recent meeting with Trish Denoon, who handles the administration of my books for Pitman Publishing, on the sidewalk at Covent Garden in London just so that my car wouldn't be towed away because I parked it illegally – as I was already more than forty minutes behind schedule for my meeting.

Having told you to be on time, you should also make sure that the customer follows the same rules. If you are conducting business below the level of board of directors or senior management you will know that customers are notorious for playing petty little games (the more senior business people don't have the time to be bothered!)

I have arrived early for appointments, unintentionally, hoping that the meeting could start ahead of schedule – which could also mean finishing ahead of schedule – only to be kept waiting until the original appointment time. True, there are times when the customer has really been too busy to interrupt what was going on to see me until the agreed time, but these situations are in the minority. This is usually a little game to allow the customer to keep the upper hand. I have also observed that on the odd occasion when I have arrived a little late for an appointment, these customers keep me waiting almost exactly the same time that I was late!

When customers play these games it usually means that your chances of winning the business are not very good, so with that in mind you should adopt a more assertive strategy, but for goodness sake don't confuse assertiveness with aggressiveness.

To illustrate what you should do in these situations I would like to relate an experience that I had when working with one of my clients. First let me explain that when I am working with clients' sales forces I become involved in three main areas of field accompaniment:

1 When I make joint calls with a member of the sales team in order to help me to understand the culture of the business.

2 When I make joint calls with a member of the sales team to ensure the implementation of what I have taught.

3 When I accompany sales managers who are making joint calls with their people.

In the third type of situation, I don't go in to the customer's premises with the manager and sales person. It would make the customer feel uncomfortable if three of us descended on her or him in a sales call and the real purpose of my presence is to observe how the manager handles the sales person after each call – the 'kerbside conference'.

Some time ago I was making joint visits with a sales manager and one of his sales people. It had been a successful day and we had arrived at our last call around 5.30 pm. I went for a coffee to await their return. I went back about half an hour later to see that the manager and the sales person were still waiting in reception to be seen. I moved across the road to where I could see but not be seen (like some demented private detective) and spent a further fifteen minutes, during which they were still kept waiting. I adjourned to the nearest coffee bar to await developments. Another fifteen minutes later I returned to the customer's premises to see the manager and the sales person finally being shown in to see the customer. They came out after half an hour and I joined them as they were walking back towards the car. When we met, I said, 'You didn't get any business in there did you?' and they both replied to the effect that not only was I correct but that the meeting had been an absolute waste of time as the customer had tried to railroad them into all sorts of discounts on products and back up services without giving them any opportunity to present the new product, for which the appointment had been arranged in the first place.

I went on to explain my thinking about customers who play games and how this particular one had shown contempt for the value of their time. Experience told me, before they even got in to see the customer, that they would be coming out empty-handed. The sales manager asked, 'What should we have done in that situation?' My reply to them is one that I would stand by in any similar situation, 'If the customer had explained that due to an emergency he wouldn't be able to see you for some time, you should have rearranged the appointment. If you had simply been kept waiting, as you had, after twenty minutes you should have explained that you were running into time problems for another meeting and would have to leave, requesting an alternative appointment. Whether you got the new appointment or not – YOU SHOULD HAVE LEFT!'

113

Winning commitment – including 'closing the sale'

I deliberately refer to winning commitment because you will often find yourself in the situation where you can't close the sale, simply because your discussions with your customer have not yet reached that stage. But you would always want to win commitment to the next stage of the sale.

What might some of these stages be?

1   A test of some kind on your products, perhaps to check specification, operating conditions, etc.

2   A small trial order to see how your company performs.

3　A sample being submitted to see how well it fits in to the customer's business.

4　A visit to your offices, sites or factories to see the type of company that you represent.

5　A follow-up meeting to make a presentation of your recommendations.

Finally, however, you will need to take the bit between your teeth and ASK FOR THE ORDER!

The problem that most of us have with this is that it is the final great opportunity that the customer has to say NO! so we 'beat about the bush' hoping that the customer will offer the order. As a result of this a whole series of 'closing techniques' have been developed over the years, by people in the training profession, to make it easier for you to do so.

The simple fact of life is that from the moment you meet the customer, your whole attitude and demeanour should be that you are practising **the A B C of closing**: **A**lways **B**e **C**losing!

While on the subject of closing, there is another piece of nonsense that has been created by my profession: **the trial close!**

There is no such thing as a trial close! A trial close is simply a close that didn't work! We delude ourselves that this is a genuine technique. You ask for the order and you either get it, in which case it is a successful close or you don't get it in which case we prefer to say that it was a trial close than that it was an unsuccessful close!

Some of the 'closing techniques' do have some validity, so I have reproduced here the most common ones and leave you to judge which are better or worse. If they work for you, use them; if they don't, treat them with the contempt that they deserve. They are in no order of importance and the suggestions will need to be adapted to your own business situation. You may also find that you have heard some of these various 'closes' under different names. The names are less important than the techniques themselves, so give them any name that reminds you what to do.

I've said it before and I offer no apologies for repeating myself: From the moment you walk in the door you are closing the sale!

The Basic or Direct Close

- Ask for the order!
- 'Shall we go ahead then?'
- 'Will you give me your order?'
- 'From what you've said can I take it that you would like to place an order?'

There comes a time when you have to take the bull by the horns and risk the rejection – ask for the order or you could die wondering!

The Alternative Close

- 'Do you want it delivered or would you prefer to collect?'
- 'Shall we deliver to the various offices or do you want it all delivered to headquarters?'
- 'Do you want it at the end of this month or the beginning of next month?'
- 'Would you like it in black or do you prefer it in brown?'

This close changes the decision in the customer's mind from 'Will I or won't I buy..?' to 'Which will I buy?'

The Assumptive Close

- 'We'll have the work completed before the end of next week!'
- 'You'll find that we will complete the installation in plenty of time for the opening!'
- 'We'll start on Monday and have the job finished before the end of the week!'

This one is my personal favourite. If you have conducted the sales call as recommended in this book, the order should be the natural conclusion to your discussion. So assume that you will get it and you'll be surprised how often you do.

The Sincerity Close

- 'What do you want us to do to become one of your preferred suppliers?'
- 'What do I need to do to get your business?'

There may be times when you appear to be up against a brick wall. Ask the question, you have nothing left to lose. I remember running a training course for sales people in the car leasing business during which one of the participants took this close one stage further and told me that he had actually 'begged' for the order. I wouldn't ever recommend that you go that far and I could certainly never bring myself to do it, but apparently he got the order – so who's right?

The Reduction Close

'Would you like to order a hundred or would you prefer the initial order to be fifty?'
'Will we go ahead with the three different sizes or would you prefer to begin with only two?'

This close is similar to the assumptive in that the decision isn't 'Should I buy?' but 'How much should I buy?' It also gives the customer the opportunity to be conservative and begin with a smaller commitment.

The Fear Close

- 'If you don't place the order now, we won't be able to deliver the stock in time for Christmas!'
From the insurance industry:

- 'If something happens to you before we arrange adequate insurance, how well will your family cope?' or,
- 'If I leave here tonight without making sure that you are adequately insured and something happens to you tomorrow, what will happen to your family?'

I even remember an insurance salesman taking this one stage further to the point that it could almost be called the 'terror' close: he said, 'If you had died before I got here tonight, what kind of mess would you have left your family in?'

I have to warn you that many people will take exception to this kind of bullying so if you decide to use this close, do so with extreme caution. Personally, I have never used it – even when selling insurance!

The Impending Event Close

- 'If you make the decision now you will still be able to take advantage of the tax relief in this financial year.'
- 'If you go ahead now we will be able to have all of the equipment in place before your official opening.'
- 'By ordering now you will be able to beat the price increase which comes into effect at the end of the month.'

117

This is almost a fear close but it is used in such a way as to make it considerably more acceptable.

The Special Event Close

- 'This month we are offering our complete range of compact saloon cars with interest free financing.'
- 'We are offering free battery charging kits with all portable telephones delivered before the end of this month.'
- 'We are offering free installation on all kitchens supplied and fitted before the end of next month.'

This can be a really good close, mainly because your company wouldn't have the special event if it wasn't meant to be used to increase sales. The only danger is that a really astute buyer will reckon that if it can be done this month it can also be done next month and will try to bargain with you at a later date. I know I use that 'buying' technique all the time – and it works.

The Concession Close

This is almost a variation on the special event close but with a subtle difference, the special offer isn't available to everyone.

- 'If you order the dictation equipment today I'll make sure that we give you a free box of cassettes to go with each machine.'

This close can be used in any situation where consumables are involved: paper or toner with laser printers or photocopiers; batteries with any kind of portable 'electrical' equipment like pagers, 'phones, etc; ribbons with typewriters, etc.

The Reverse Question or Tunaround Close

This should be used in the situation where the customer asks a specific question, such as, 'Can I have it in black?' Your response should be 'Would you like it in black?' Another example would be where the customer says, 'When could you deliver?' and you reply 'When would you like it delivered?'

When the customer asks this type of question it is often mere curiosity, the reverse question focuses the attention and goes for real commitment.

The Sharp Angle Close

This is a variation on the above and I have only kept it separate because it is considerably more direct. The customer may say something like, 'Can you deliver inside two weeks?' Your reply would be 'If I can deliver inside two weeks will you give me the order now?' That's what I call closing the sale!

The Secondary Question Close

I have seen this one used to great effect in situations where payment was to be made by regular monthly bank debits: 'When is the best time of the month for the Direct Debit to be drawn from your bank account?' or, 'What invoice address do you use?'

This is asking for the order in a slightly oblique fashion where you really ask a much less direct question but within which it is implicit that the order would be signed.

The Puppy Dog Close

This is when what you have to offer is so good that you would leave it and let the customer try it. You then return at a pre-arranged time confident that, having used the product the customer won't want to give it back, you have a sale! This technique was used with considerable success in the late 1960s in the UK when colour television was introduced. The TV rental companies offered a seven-day free trial of a colour television. They almost invariably installed the trial TVs just before the weekend and consequently their engineers and sales people called back – just before the new weekend was about to begin – to take these back. The only way that the customers could get to keep them, with the weekend looming large, was to sign a rental agreement. The success rate was phenomenally high. Who wanted to go back to watching monochrome television having experienced full colour? The technique was again used with almost equal success during the introduction of video cassette recorders.

119

I was conducting a training programme with a large refrigeration company when I was asked to explain how this close came to have its name. It was from the practice of people who bred and sold pedigree dogs. At the time when mum, dad and the children, came to view the puppies the breeder would take this absolutely loveable little dog and give it to one of the children. After a couple of minutes when everyone had fallen in love with this sweet little animal, the breeder would advise the price. Irrespective of whether it was regarded as expensive or not, there was no way that the children concerned were going to give up the puppy. Poor old mum and dad were well and truly hooked. The sale was made!

It transpired that the reason that I had been asked to explain how the technique came to be named was that the questioner, Robert Campbell, was a breeder of Pomeranian dogs. Robert was one of the sales people with that refrigeration company and over the years since then has become one of my closest friends. He is currently the sales director of Atholl Refrigeration in Scotland and is an extremely professional, likeable and successful businessman. He told me later that he had used the 'puppy dog close' to such effect that he increased the selling price of his dogs yet still managed to sell all of them with no difficulty whatsoever.

If you have a product or service that is so good that the customer will not want to give it up after having experienced it – use the puppy dog close. If your product or service doesn't fall into that category, try another close – the puppy dog close might simply postpone the decision.

The Objection Close

Cast your mind back to Chapter 6 when we looked at the objection handling technique.

- 'If I can satisfy you regarding that...?'
- 'If I can satisfy you regarding that situation can we talk serious business?'
- 'If I can show you how to overcome that problem will you give us your business?'

The Duke of Wellington/The Winston Churchill/ The Balance Sheet Close

The story goes (or should I say myth) that both the Duke of Wellington and Winston Churchill had the habit, before making an important decision, of writing on a sheet of paper all of the reasons why the decision should go one way and then all the reasons why it should go another way. Whichever was the longest list determined what the decision would be. If you believe that you'll believe anything!

I have heard it probably more accurately referred to as the balance sheet close where you ask the customer to write on the left-hand side of a piece of paper all of the reasons why he or she would not buy your product or service or alternatively why they would buy a competitor's product or service. You then take the piece of paper and in discussion with the customer write on the right-hand side of the paper all of the reasons why he or she should buy your product or service, the thinking being that the longest list will win and as you are helping the customer to compile the list in your favour – you will win!

What a load of nonsense! I have never seen it used to effect and I couldn't bring myself to use something so obviously manipulative and insulting to the customer's intelligence. I only reproduce it here because I still hear sales people refer to it. If you find that it works for you, please write to me because I would love to know.

121

The Fear of Rejection Close

This is the one to use when you're terrified that a closed or direct question will invite a negative reply.

- 'What would prevent you from going ahead today?'

It works but it is a bit on the soft side. There may be situations that are so tentative that you would fall back on this, but it is much more character-building to just ask for the order.

The 'Not Dead Yet' Close

There will be situations where the customer will tell you that he or she wants to think about it! You need to double check that this isn't simply an excuse and ask questions like:

- 'What is it exactly that I haven't fully explained?'
- 'Which part of my proposal is it that you need to think about?'

Any way of making sure that the customer has all the information – and understands it all – to be able to make a considered decision. This also enables you to pull the situation back to where you may be able to make your presentation again and close the sale. However, there will be times when the customer will insist on wanting to think about it.

To try to retrieve the situation before you leave, make a return appointment so that you can come back when the customer has had time to think about it. Close your diary or briefcase and prepare to leave. The customer has now begun to relax. When you get to the door, say, 'You know, Mr Smith, in situations like this I usually find that when I come back next week you will have decided against going ahead with my recommendations!' If the customer tells you that this is true, you say, 'In that case, why don't you tell me now why that is and we can dispense with the need for another appointment?' If the customer says that he or she won't make a negative decision, say, 'Why don't we spend a few more minutes together to see if we can resolve the situation now?' If the customer insists that there needs to be thinking time, you have already made the return appointment. Thank him or her politely and say that you look forward to next week's meeting.

There is always the possibility in this situation that, having relaxed, the customer may be prepared to re-enter the discussion and you will get the opportunity to close the sale there and then. I am not particularly fond of this close although I have used it very effectively. The only problem I find is that I am not totally comfortable with it – it just isn't me.

I gave this as an example of a closing technique on a recent training programme and when the next stage of the training came around one of the participants told me of a situation where he had used it and it had worked. He also told me that the style of this close was compatible with his style and personality and he felt very comfortable using it. So let me reiterate: if any of these work for you – use them!

However you use any or all of these techniques, the truism is that if you don't ASK FOR THE ORDER, you run the risk that you won't get it!

CALL IT WHAT IT IS!

I was recently on the receiving end of a closing technique which could best be described as a combination of the impending event close and the special event close.

I had gone to test drive a top-of-the-range German saloon car and having driven it was sufficiently impressed to ask for more details. The first thing I was told was that they had a special offer available – if I took delivery of the car within the month. This amounted to the fact that the cars which were available had all been fitted out with some £2000 worth of extras. I was then informed that the reason that I had to take delivery of the car within the month was that a model was being introduced which had some 'minor cosmetic' changes.

123

This is motor trade speak to explain that any similarity between the old model and the new would be almost accidental; in short I would be buying a noticeably dated car. Finally I was told that the figure that they would offer me in part exchange for the Swedish car I was handing over as part of the deal was such that it appeared to be some £1500 more than I knew the car's true value to be. A good deal you might think! However, for reasons not explained, they would need to present the figures on paper in a slightly different way. The net result was that in real terms I would be buying a 'dated' model with extras which had been 'thrown in' by the manufacturer to get rid of this old stock before the introduction of the new model, in a colour that I preferred not to have (there was only one colour choice available) and that when the figures added up I was really getting around £2000 less than I knew my Swedish car to be worth. If any degree of honesty had prevailed I would have been in a position to negotiate but as it was I knew that I was being railroaded into an extremely unfavourable deal for me – but certainly not the car dealer. If he had been honest with me I may have gone back to try to renegotiate the deal but as it was I opted for an entirely different car from an altogether different source – and all because he wouldn't call it what it was – a chance to buy a good motor car at a good price because they had a number left over that they needed to get rid of within a certain time period!

This happened to me in my native Scotland and reminded me of the famous quotation attributed to JM Barrie, the author of *Peter Pan*, 'There is nothing quite as impressive as a Scotsman on the make!'

Whatever you do in business call it what it is because if the customer ever finds out that you told less than the truth – you're dead with no chance of ever doing business there again!

THE POWER OF COMMITMENT

Winning commitment from any customer, particularly to buying your products, should give you a great feeling; not one of having conquered but one of having reached an agreement and possibly an understanding. As important is the fact that it records another landmark in building up your relationship with your customer.

If you cast your mind back to Chapter 1 you will recall that we looked at some of the things which customers take into consideration when making decisions and the emotion which can be involved in the buyer/ seller relationship. This commitment, however, can manifest itself in ways you wouldn't expect as I would like to relate in the following story.

A number of years ago when I was working with a large training organisation, that company had the habit of staging 'Open Day' seminars to which they invited existing customers and prospective customers so that they could be introduced to some of the different types of training being carried out with other companies. These 'open days' were free of charge to the participants, but the only condition was that should anyone, who had agreed to attend, cancel with less than seven days' notice or simply not turn up, there would be a cancellation fee of £25 to offset the costs associated with their non-attendance, for example lunch, refreshments, etc. which had to be ordered in advance.

On just such an occasion at the Sheraton Hotel in Edinburgh I had invited an existing customer, Richard F Cummings, who was and, at the time of writing, still is, the personnel director of a major international engineering company on the outskirts of Glasgow. As I waited in the lobby of the Sheraton, Dick arrived just before the starting time and in response to my question, 'How's business?', stated that he was so busy that it would really have suited him to 'call off' from attending the day.

125

My rejoinder was that I would have understood if he had not arrived. At this point he looked me straight in the eye and said, 'Have you any idea how it feels to authorise an invoice for something you haven't done?'

Dick Cummings, now OBE, is the consummate personnel professional and one of the most likeable, albeit hard-nosed, businessmen I have ever met. In terms of having to do business with him, he is a major player who, deliberately or otherwise, would intimidate many a sales person. Dick doesn't balk at authorising payments of many thousands of pounds, but he didn't want to pay £25 for something he hadn't done.

It obviously wasn't the money; it was the **principle** which was involved. Winning commitment from a customer, however insignificant that may seem at the time, is an extremely powerful thing to achieve, even if it is only the commitment to meeting again.

So, even if you don't get an order today, try to win commitment to something!

CHECKLIST – CHAPTER 8

■ Make sure that you create a good initial impression – sell yourself!

■ Remember the three 'twelves'.

■ Sell first and leave the pleasantries till the end.

■ Be enthusiastic!

■ Winning commitment includes 'closing the sale', but would also be winning commitment to the next stage in the process.

■ Ask for the order – in any way that works for you.

■ Practise the A B C of closing.

■ Never mind the nonsense you've heard, there is no such thing as a trial close – a trial close is simply a close that didn't work!

■ From the moment you walk in the door you are closing the sale!

■ Don't pull the wool over the customer's eyes – call it what it is!

■ Never underestimate the power of commitment.

■ If you don't get an order today – win commitment to something!

9

The complete sale

In this chapter I would like to very quickly put the complete process in place after which I will spend some time answering some of the questions that sales people ask me – to show you how to maintain lasting impressions.

The golden rules for effective sales calls

Remember the difference between efficient and effective: **'Efficient'** is doing things properly and **'Effective'** is doing the proper things. Let's make sure that you do the proper things:

1 Make sure that you have a clearly defined objective for each and every sales call.

2 Any presentation or recommendation that you make must be based on the customer's understanding and perception of the situation.

3 Ask questions and take time to listen to the answers.

4 Satisfy the customer that what you have to offer will meet his or her needs.

5 Uncover all of the objections and handle them to the customer's satisfaction.

6 Keep the initiative.

7 Close on your objective.

The steps of the sale

We will now go through the steps of the sale but first you need to recognise that there are three distinct types of call:

1 The 'Hunting' Call

When you are breaking new ground. This could be with an existing customer when you are trying to sell another part of your range or a new product or service that has been introduced by your company. It could be with an infrequent buyer of your goods and services and you are trying to establish a more permanent relationship so that they become one of your regular buying customers. It will most often be when you are trying to sell to an entirely new prospect.

2 The 'Follow Up' Call

When you are in any stage of the 'hunting' situation where you have been unable to secure the decision on the first call and have to re-visit in order to close the sale.

3 The 'Farming' Call

This is when you are working with your existing customer base, building relationships, securing repeat business, keeping the competition at bay, increasing your share of the potential business, etc.

As you go through the steps that I outline please bear in mind that you won't go through every step on every call, but that within the framework provided you will be able to ensure that you keep control. I will give you the main outline under 'The Hunting Call' and point out the differences as we go through the others.

The hunting call

Gain information from observation

Look for things that will increase your knowledge of the situation:

- Signs of competitive activity.
- The type of business that it is.

- Whether the company seems busy or quiet.
- Whether it is a prosperous looking business.
- The kind of cars that are in the car park, etc.

Be careful, however, not to assume too much. If you see something of interest bring it into the conversation and check its validity. I once had an insurance sales person visit me at home and during our conversation he kept coming round to the subject of young children. At that time I was a bit past my 'shelf-life' for having really young children although marginally on the young side to be a grandparent, but for some peculiar reason this man kept coming back to things that would relate to children. As he was getting absolutely nowhere with this line of conversation he, obviously in exasperation (or was it desperation), asked whose children lived in my home. I told him that there were none and asked where he had picked up that idea. His reply was quite refreshing in that he told me he had noticed a number of children's rubber 'squeaky' toys in the garden and driveway. He almost got it right – there is a real 'baby' in my home: a cocker spaniel called Jade. They were her toys!

129

Introduce Yourself and Your Company and State the Purpose of your Meeting

Introducing yourself means slightly more than stating your name. Tell the customer who you are, for example, 'My name is Jane Smith and I am the sales executive in this area representing the A B C Telephone company'. The same with your company; say what it does and introduce anything special about it, for example, 'A B C Telephones are the authorised distributors in this part of England for X Y Z, the market leading Cellular telephones.' Then go on to remind the customer why you are there – he or she may have forgotten, for example, 'I telephoned you last week and arranged this meeting to discuss how our range of telephones may prove beneficial in the day to day running of your business.'

Relax the Customer and Establish the DMP (Decision-making process)

You might think that the introduction I suggest is a little abrupt, but it needs to be clear and concise. You now have an opportunity to relax the customer by introducing things like: 'I must say that your reception area is extremely tastefully decorated' or in a domestic environment, 'You really do have a beautiful home/garden.' Obviously don't ever say something like this if it is patently obvious that it isn't true!

Keep clear of things like: 'Isn't this awful weather!' – the customer knows that the weather is awful and certainly doesn't need reminding of it. Try to say something positive instead of creating an air of depression.

Similarly with sport. The customer may not be a rugby, cricket, soccer, tennis or golf fan – let him or her take the lead if that type of conversation eventually crops up.

Now that the customer is relaxed you need to establish the DMP, for example, 'If you saw something today that your company wanted, who other than yourself would be involved in that decision?' or, 'Who else would you consult before making your decision?' or 'If you wanted to place an order, what would be the system for the paperwork?'

The problem is that if your meeting isn't with the decision-maker, the chances are that the person you are talking to won't tell you. There are some clues – remarks like: 'All requisitions come through me' – likely to be a clerk processing paperwork on the basis of somebody else's decision; 'The managing director would "rubber stamp" my decision' – managing directors don't 'rubber stamp' decisions, they make them. What this person really means is that he or she will in turn present your information to the managing director, who will then make the decision.

The danger in this situation, even if the 'buyer' genuinely presents your information and doesn't simply enclose your brochures and price list in a memo to the MD, is that the only person really qualified to 'sell' your product or service is you! If you discover that you don't have the decision-maker you need to try to get to them – but this can be difficult because your original contact may feel undermined or threatened, so you have to be careful. Try something like, 'Perhaps when we have had our discussion we could both have a quick word with the MD in case he or she has any particular questions which I could answer while I'm here?'

It won't always work, but you need to try every way you can to get to the decision-maker – even if it means coming back when you can arrange a joint meeting.

The best way to overcome these situations is to try to make sure that they don't happen in the first place. Do some better quality research into your prospect before you make the appointment to make sure that you get to the real 'buyer'.

131

Whether or not you are with the real decision-maker follow the next step.

Get the Customer to Want to Answer Questions

You are now into 'Digging for Gold' but I will produce all of the steps here to reinforce the structure.

Begin with General Open Questions

Based on the answers to the general questions, continue.

Continue with Specific Open and Closed Questions

Summarise the Customer's Needs and Desires
Ask the Final Question, 'Is There Anything Else...?'

Make Your Presentation

Ask for the Order

Now we get to the panic when the customer raises an objection.

Objections

Use the objection handling technique which you have from Chapter 6.

Pause

Get more information.

Tell Me More!

Get even more information.

'Apart from That...?'

Get all of the objections out in the open.

'If I can Satisfy You Regarding That...?'

Go for commitment if you can handle the objection(s).

Present Your Answer

Make it a good one!

'Are You Satisfied with That?'

Check that the customer agrees that it answers the objection.

Win Commitment to the next stage or close the sale

Get agreement to the trial, test, sample, factory visit, return appointment, etc.

Ask for the order.

The follow up call

Gain Information from Observation

Things may have changed since you last called.

Confirm the Purpose of the Meeting

Whatever the agreement you reached, whether it was to get a decision or make a presentation of your recommendations, remind the customer why you are there.

Relax the Customer and Re-Establish the DMP

When you relax the customer, try to remember what you said last time and don't talk about a tastefully decorated reception or a beautiful house or garden – again. It tends to give the game away that you've been practising! As far as the DMP is concerned, check if anything has changed and react accordingly.

Summarise the Last Meeting

Remind the customer what the situation was when you last met. You're going to look pretty stupid if you re-launch straight into 'Digging for Gold'. But you will want to make sure that the situation that you left is still current, so get back into general open questions.

133

General Open Questions

Kick-start it with something along the lines of, 'Before I go on to tell you what my company recommends that you do, I would like to double check a couple of points for my own understanding.'

Use the Specific Open and Closed Questions

If you're still reading this book you are taking this subject as seriously as I had hoped and you have managed to 'sneak' back into 'Digging for Gold' without anyone really noticing.

Reconfirm the Needs and Desires

You can't take the chance of assuming that nothing has changed. I'm sorry if I seem to be going on about this, but the number of times in my early career that I have blundered into situations without checking only to find that I was wrong, still brings a glow of embarrassment to my cheeks!

Check 'Is There Anything Else?'

Present Your Recommendations

Ask for the Order!

After this point the steps are identical to those produced for the Hunting Call.

The farming call

Gain Information from Observation

Even with your regular customers, things may have changed since you last called. The competition may have made headway during your absence; there may be an expansion programme underway; the place may be unusually quiet due to short time working or reduction of the labour force, etc.

State the Purpose of the Meeting

It's too easy to fall into the trap of thinking that everything is comfortable and end up calling in for a cup of coffee with no real purpose to the meeting. This step not only ensures that your meeting has a purpose but that you also make it clear to the customer.

Relax the Customer and Re-Establish the DMP

By this time you should know the customer well enough to get involved in something a bit more meaningful than the lovely house or reception area, just be careful that it doesn't become twenty minutes of social chit-chat and twenty seconds on the way out of the door of, 'I don't suppose you wanted to order anything today?' As far as the DMP is concerned, always check if anything has changed and react accordingly.

Summarise the Situation to Date

When dealing with regular customers it does a power of good to remind them of how well your relationship is working; the business that has been done; the little problems that have been overcome; in fact all of the things that go towards a successful buyer/seller relationship. You will also have created the 'springboard' from which you can launch your bid for a bigger share of the customer's business.

To progress this call more meaningfully than perhaps you have in the past, try something like, 'John, we've been doing business for so long now that sometimes things change and we overlook them because it doesn't appear to affect what it is that we do. Would you mind if I brought myself up to date to keep myself abreast of developments?' You're back into 'Digging for Gold.'

135

General Open Questions

Then Specific Open and Closed Questions

Summarise the Needs and Desires

This may be confirmation of what you both already knew, but it won't suffer for being stated. On the other hand, if anything has changed it's a whole new ball game.

Check 'Is There Anything Else?'

Present Your Recommendations

This will be for what you should do to continue your splendid working relationship even if all that means is more of the same. You need to go through the process to remind the customer why he decided to buy from you in the first place or you leave yourself vulnerable to the competition.

If it's appropriate, then go on to the next step.

Ask for the Order!

After this point the steps are identical to those produced for the Hunting and Follow Up Calls.

I have reproduced here a diagram for each of the types of call so that you may note it in your diary and carry it with you into your calls.

I have used these for some years and I have found that as well as being an invaluable aid when I am selling, they are extremely useful when the meeting with the customer is interrupted. I use an A5-sized loose-leaf diary and have the diagrams inside the back cover, where I also keep paper for making notes. Should my meeting be interrupted, I close my diary until the interruption is over. I keep my index finger at the step of the sale where the interruption took place and when the meeting resumes I am able, with the aid of my notes, to summarise where we were so that we can pick up the meeting and carry on to a successful conclusion.

You will see that these diagrams read from the bottom up. This is deliberate to create the impression of climbing the steps to success.

Lasting impressions

In the last chapter we looked at how to create a good first impression. If you managed to create that right first impression I would like to help you make it a lasting one by addressing the most common questions that I get when running training programmes.

WIN COMMITMENT / CLOSE

ARE YOU SATISFIED WITH THAT?

PRESENT YOUR ANSWER

'IF I CAN SATISFY YOU REGARDING THAT...?'

'APART FROM THAT...?'

TELL ME MORE!

PAUSE

OBJECTIONS

ASK FOR THE ORDER

MAKE YOUR PRESENTATION

'IS THERE ANYTHING ELSE?'

SUMMARISE NEEDS AND DESIRES

SPECIFIC OPEN & CLOSED QUESTIONS

GENERAL OPEN QUESTIONS

GET THE CUSTOMER TO WANT TO ANSWER QUESTIONS

RELAX THE CUSTOMER & ESTABLISH THE DMP

OWN INTRODUCTION & PURPOSE OF THE MEETING

GAIN INFORMATION FROM OBSERVATION

Fig 9.1 'Hunting' sales calls

WIN COMMITMENT / CLOSE

ARE YOU SATISFIED WITH THAT?

PRESENT YOUR ANSWER

'IF I CAN SATISFY YOU REGARDING THAT...?'

'APART FROM THAT...?'

TELL ME MORE!

PAUSE

OBJECTIONS

ASK FOR THE ORDER

PRESENT YOUR RECOMMENDATIONS

'IS THERE ANYTHING ELSE?'

RECONFIRM NEEDS AND DESIRES

SPECIFIC OPEN & CLOSED QUESTIONS

GENERAL OPEN QUESTIONS

SUMMARISE LAST MEETING

RELAX THE CUSTOMER & RE-ESTABLISH THE DMP

CONFIRM PURPOSE OF THE MEETING

GAIN INFORMATION FROM OBSERVATION

Fig 9.2 'Follow up' sales calls

WIN COMMITMENT / CLOSE

ARE YOU SATISFIED WITH THAT?

PRESENT YOUR ANSWER

'IF I CAN SATISFY YOU REGARDING THAT...?'

'APART FROM THAT...?'

TELL ME MORE!

PAUSE

OBJECTIONS

ASK FOR THE ORDER

PRESENT YOUR RECOMMENDATIONS

'IS THERE ANYTHING ELSE?'

SUMMARISE NEEDS AND DESIRES

SPECIFIC OPEN & CLOSED QUESTIONS

GENERAL OPEN QUESTIONS

SUMMARISE SITUATION TO DATE

RELAX THE CUSTOMER & RE-ESTABLISH THE DMP

STATE PURPOSE OF THE MEETING

GAIN INFORMATION FROM OBSERVATION

139

Fig 9.3 'Farming' sales calls

The questions sales people ask!

APPEARANCE

Men

Wear a suit

Never mind the separate (and usually unco-ordinated) jacket and trousers, you're not going for a quiet beer at your local pub. It's sloppy and unprofessional. In the UK a suit still the accepted professional dress. In some European countries it may be so unusual as to make you stand out from the crowd – in a very positive manner. Polish your shoes – all over. Peter Mottram, who is now with Armitage Shanks, but with whom I worked when he was the UK national sales manager for one of the world's leading contact lens manufacturers, once told me that the last thing a customer saw was the back of your heels so always make sure that they are polished too. Not only was Peter Mottram one of the best and most professional sales managers I ever met, he is one of a very few role models I would recommend for anyone who wants to dress like a businessman.

I have worked with sales people who sell to farmers and they still wear suits even when they wear wellington boots to walk around the farm!

Try to exercise a little taste when choosing ties and shirts. If you can't, get the woman in your life to choose them for you. Sorry for the sexist remark, but women normally have much better dress sense than men.

Before I go on to address the ladies, let me return to suits; the top sales people don't wear suits from 'multiple retailers', they wear better quality and obviously more expensive suits. If you want to really make it in this business, make the extra effort, it will be a sound investment.

If you're not convinced, imagine you are being visited by a salesman who appears at your home as if he had dressed for

140

a special occasion – how would you feel, thinking that the extra effort had been made for you? Customers also want to do business with successful people, after all what you are selling must be good if you can afford to dress really well. They notice your dress and it matters.

Ladies

You have a great deal more latitude in your dress than men, but if you want to be taken seriously – and it is regrettably still a problem in some business circles even today – you have to dress accordingly. As I've said, women usually have better natural dress sense than men, but remember that you are dressing for professional meetings and not for an evening out.

There isn't a great deal more that I can say to the ladies, because my personal experience is that the majority of you know how to dress for business.

141

FIRST NAMES

If you want to build up a serious relationship with a customer it is made more difficult if you continue to refer to the customer as Mr, Mrs, Miss or Ms.

In addition, there can be a problem with some of your female customers who for professional reasons have retained their original surnames despite being married. Michèle Martin of Roche is actually Mrs Yates, but if she was to be introduced to you as 'Martin' and you observed her engagement and wedding rings you could easily fall into the trap of referring to her as Mrs Martin – which she is not.

So when do you call a customer by his or her first name?

1   When the customer introduces herself or himself by the first name.

2   When you are given a business card which shows the first name.

3   When you are invited to do so by the customer.

4   When the customer refers to you by your first name.

How can you encourage the use of first names?

1   Always introduce yourself by your first name.

2   Make sure that it is printed on your business card.

You will usually find this is enough to encourage the use of first names throughout the conversation.

Probably the only time that it could become a problem is when there is a really significant age gap between you and the customer, for example, when the customer is much older and you are still quite young. One of the advantages of getting to my age is that you're old enough to call anybody what you like!

ALCOHOL

It goes without saying that if you are in charge of a motor vehicle – DON'T! Beyond that I don't think that it's as clear cut as some would suggest.

Even if you don't drive, I would advise against drinking during the day unless it is a business lunch with a customer. This can be a good way to build on your relationship with your customer, but if you become involved in this, don't visit other customers afterwards. They won't like the smell of alcohol on your breath and even if you explain that you have been to a business lunch with a customer, they will wonder why you haven't ever taken them.

The one exception I have noticed, and even that is on the decrease, is when selling to the licensed trade where the culture for many years has been to share a beer with the landlord or landlady of the establishment. When I was selling to that trade many years ago I eventually had to become a teetotaller because if I hadn't I would have been 'out of my mind' by three o'clock every afternoon.

'SLEEPING WITH THE ENEMY'

What I am about to say here applies irrespective of gender.

Perhaps it is surprising, but I am asked this question more often than most of the others. It is one which I have seldom found anyone in my position prepared to address unless they simply take a high moral stance. I don't intend to do that but my position is quiet clear – **never do it**!

The reasons why I say you should never do it are all based on good business sense:

1　This section is called 'sleeping with the enemy' for the very simple reason that this is what your customer will eventually become if you get involved – an enemy!

2　Once you start sleeping with the customer, whether it was originally to get the business or not, you will have to keep sleeping with the customer or you will lose the business.

3　You will introduce into the business a level of emotion that you can't control. This business can be hard enough without laying minefields for yourself for a later date.

4　You don't know who else in the customer's company would like to be sleeping with that person and who will eventually make sure that life becomes extremely difficult for you.

5　If someone in the customer's company finds out – and these things have a habit of being found out – your business may well come under the kind of scrutiny that it can't withstand.

6　Even if it can withstand that scrutiny, there must be a conflict of interests.

7　It is called 'screwing your own business!' Actually it's called something else but I would never get away with putting into print what it's really called.

There you are, seven good reasons why you should never 'sleep with the enemy' and not one of them from a moral viewpoint. At the end of the day I wouldn't care to pass judgement. As long as you aren't 'screwing my business' it has nothing to do with me, I have merely tried to answer a question which many before me have chosen to avoid.

Handling rejection

Sales people are the most resilient group of individuals that I have ever met. What other group of people would choose to spend their working lives subjecting themselves to rejection on a daily basis?

None I suspect. So how do you manage it or, if you are having difficulty, how can you manage it?

144

I have observed something really strange over the years about many top sales people – they are not as outrageously extrovert as some would at first imagine! In fact some of the best sales people I have ever known were really quite insecure. So in these cases, how do they handle rejection?

It's a performance

Look at all of the best sales people you know. They are just like actors – and you never met a more insecure bunch than that in your life. The top sales people crave attention. They are raconteurs and comedians. They know a myriad of stories many of which become increasingly embellished with every telling. They have a thousand anecdotes about their successes and conveniently forget their failures.

The top sales people have adopted a role that they play with great effect. Some of this is based on what they are and some is based on what they would like to be. Who else do you know who could create a hilarious cabaret around something personal, and often painful, like a vasectomy operation, childbirth or a divorce?

When one of these people is rejected on a frequent basis, it isn't the person who is being rejected – it's the performance which wasn't good enough on the day. Not for them the moaning and complaining about poor products and services or poor customer care on the part of their company. They go back to the basics and improve their levels of knowledge and skill in order to improve the performance and gradually reduce the amount of rejection.

Show me a top sales person who wins an order during the first call of the day and I will show you a sales person who is unstoppable for the rest of the day. It's why so many of them deliberately set out their plan for the day to begin with a call that they refer to as a 'banker' – as certain a prospect as you can get!

I have held this theory for some time and every time I get into conversation with good sales people about it, there are knowing looks and almost imperceptible nods of agreement.

145

Even if what I have said is wrong, go back to the basics and improve your levels of knowledge and skill and you will improve your sales performance and you will reduce the incidence of rejection and it will become manageable.

CHECKLIST – CHAPTER 9

■ Study and remember the golden rules for effective sales calls.

■ Identify the three types of call and learn the structures for carrying them through from start to finish.

■ Make sure that you create the right lasting impression.

■ When you dress for business – be better than the rest.

■ Build up relationships through the use of first names.

■ Be circumspect in relation to alcohol when you're working.

■ Never 'Sleep with the Enemy'!

■ Learn to handle and minimise rejection by going back to basics and improving your performance.

10

Body language in the sales call

Over the years, much has been written about body language, the unconscious or subconscious gestures that we all make that give away our true feelings. It's a subject that can take up a lot of time on a training programme because it isn't enough to describe it – it has to be demonstrated as well. I somehow get the feeling that the fascination with the subject is due, in the main, to the sales person's desire to create some kind of magic wand that can be waved so that everything turns out perfectly!

There have been many splendid, and some not so splendid, books written on the subject so in this chapter I would like to spend time only on the body language that is of value in the selling situation – both yours and the customer's. I will not be dwelling on that part which is reputed to be extremely useful when trying to attract the attention of members of the opposite sex, nor will I spend any time on the history and background of how it is supposed to have come about. I am only interested here in its effective use in selling situations.

Body language is reputed to be responsible for between sixty per cent and eighty per cent of the message that a person conveys! This means that even unconsciously we judge people by what their bodies say more than we do by the words that they utter.

If there is a 'secret' to reading body language it is in the fact that body movements and gestures should not be read in isolation, in much the same way that you wouldn't take words out of context and expect them to have any real meaning. Rather than concentrate on the 'signals' being sent and give you examples of the body language which could convey that message, I would prefer to look at the body movements and then try to translate these into something meaningful. It's the body movement you will notice first.

Always bear in mind as you read through this, however, that body language is not an exact science! For that reason there are a few situations where there are alternative 'readings'.

The customer's body language: Understanding and responding to it

The customer who stares, has parted lips and a finger placed on the teeth is exhibiting **anxiety.**

Say: 'You're not looking too happy, what have I said that concerns you?'

The customer whose body is confrontational, leaning towards you with either the head or the jaw jutted is trying to **dominate** you.

Do: Place your arms behind your head with your body slack to show that you're totally relaxed and in command of the situation.

Don't: Mirror the body language and create confrontation.

The customer who has hands on hips, pointing a finger and with firm lips is also trying to **dominate** you.

Do: Move slightly – not back – to create more body space.

Don't: Mirror the body language or move towards the customer and create confrontation.

The customer whose arms are folded across the chest and who is sitting 'bolt upright' is in **disagreement** with what you are saying. Folded arms is a classic defensive gesture.

Say: 'You don't appear too happy with what I have said, what is it that you disagree with?'

The customer who is pulling at a shirt collar – often running the index fingers around the inside of the collar is either displaying **discomfort** or **awkwardness** or is **lying**!

Say: 'You don't look too comfortable, what have I said to cause this?'

The customer who is stroking the chin or scratching the head is being **thoughtful**.

Say: 'You appear to be giving consideration to what I have said, what other information can I give you?'

The customer who is looking intently at you with the head cocked and the body totally still is being **attentive**.

Do: Carry on with what you were saying and look for other signs.

The customer who is seeking eye contact, maintaining a straight gaze, restricting the blinking and may even have the hand placed on the heart is either exhibiting **sincerity** – or deliberately trying to make you think that is the case!

Don't: Be taken in until there are other signs which help you.

The customer who is covering then rubbing the eyes or looking down or who draws the index finger across the nose horizontally is either **lying** or thinks that **you are lying**.

Say: 'What is it that I've said that you are unhappy about?'

The customer who narrows the eyelids is being **suspicious**.

Say: 'You're obviously unhappy about something, what have I said to make you feel this way?'

The customer who shrugs the shoulders is **totally indifferent.**

Say: 'I don't appear to have covered what you're looking for yet, what more can I tell you?'

The customer whose arms are behind the head with the body slack is **totally relaxed** and usually **in command of the situation**.

Do: Mirror the body language; there's no harm if it's not confrontational.

This pose is probably the one for which I am personally best known. I even have some customers where the mutual relaxation in each other's company is such that we both positively 'slouch' in armchairs during our meetings. You have read that I fell off the stage at the Holiday Inn; well, I have also come very close to falling off the chairs in some of my customers' offices.

The customer whose head is down, has eyes semi-closed with the lips set or has the head supported by the hand(s) is **bored to tears**.

Say: 'I don't appear to have caught your imagination yet, what kind of information would you like me to give you?'

The customer who is rubbing the nose is displaying **uncertainty** or **anxiety** or, if speaking, is either **lying** or **exaggerating**. Give the benefit of the doubt.

Say: 'You don't seem awfully happy with what I've said so far, what is it that is making you uneasy?'

The customer who is closing the eyes has either **fallen asleep** or is displaying **dislike of you**!

Say: (if nothing else, speaking will awaken the customer) 'There is obviously something I have said or done that you don't like, can you help me by telling me what it was?' You may as well go for broke because if you don't sort it out you may as well leave!

The customer who has clenched fists is really, really **angry**!

Say: 'I've obviously said something to upset you for which I apologise, but could you please tell me what it was?' Similar situation to the one above, it's make or break time.

The customer who is brushing specks from the knee or picking lint from clothing or washing the hands is exhibiting **disapproval** of you or what you are saying.

Say: 'You're obviously not very happy with what I've told you. Exactly what was it that you didn't like?'

The customer who has hooded the eyes, has the finger cradling the nose or the leg crossed over the knee with the hand on the ankle is giving you a **negative evaluation**.

Say: 'There is something about what I've said that hasn't exactly captured your interest, what kind of information would be of interest to you?'

The customer who discontinues the natural stance, steps back or looks down and sways before turning away from you to begin doing other work has told you that **the meeting is over**!

151

Do: Thank the customer for the time – and leave!

The customer who is leaning forward without confrontation is **interested**.

Do: Mirror the body language and get the customer more involved in what it is you're saying.

The customer who regularly touches the watch is either **short of time** or thinks that things could be moving along a bit **quicker**.

Say: 'If I can very quickly go through this with you before we run out of time and then perhaps I can arrange to come back again to finish our discussion.'

The customer who has the habit of touching and stroking inanimate objects is exhibiting **loneliness**. (Why is it on training programmes that everybody bursts out laughing when I get to this one?)

Do: Stop talking about business and start to talk about the person and his or her interests. It's probably a long time since anybody asked this person about anything other than business! If you strike up rapport on this level it won't take you long to establish a lasting business relationship.

Body language is only part of the answer. When you are with the customer there will be facial expressions which will improve your interpretation and at the end of the day, what the customer actually says to you should help to complete the whole picture.

There are many other examples of body language in the selling situation but I have tried to cover the most common ones here. There is, however, an additional one that I would like to give you and I have left it until the end because it is the most powerful example of body language that you can use with the customer.

With the exception of the confrontational ones I mentioned before, whatever pose the customer adopts, mirror the body language! Synchronise your postures with the customer's and whenever the posture changes – change with it. It is one of the most powerful and quickest ways of establishing rapport, because the unconscious message is that you are both on the same wave length. In non-business situations it is referred to as 'quasi'-courting behaviour!

Proving that body language does work!

A few years ago when I was working with Ciba Vision in the UK, I was asked to run a training programme for new recruits to get them, as quickly as possible, up to the skills level of the rest of the existing team. There were three new male recruits, one new female recruit and a member of the marketing department who was participating as part of her overall business education.

The female sales person was Mary Finn, the most delightful person and one of the most professional sales people you are ever likely to meet. It pleases me greatly to know that she has since become a member of the sales management team.

We were working in a hotel in Hampshire and at the end of the day in which I had been talking about body language, we adjourned to the bar after dinner for the usual sort of chat that takes place on these occasions.

To help you understand, Mary and the three men had spent around six weeks on induction training including intensive product training, during which time, as is extremely common, a bond had been created between them all. To improve your understanding further, I should also let you know that Mary is the most tactile person I have ever come across in my life. I am extremely tactile, but I'm not in Mary's league. We all sat and talked about business and training and all of the challenges that the future would bring and, being very intense, Mary was driving more and more of the conversation. Every time she spoke to me she touched me. Every time she wanted to draw my attention to something important she would grasp my hand. I was aware that the others were conscious of this and I deliberately launched into mirroring and synchronised posture behaviour. While I was doing this I was also able to observe the body language of the male members of the group, who regarded Mary as one of them! When the time came to close the conversation I suggested to everyone that perhaps we should start thirty minutes ahead of schedule the next day as there was an important topic that I wanted to pick up.

153

The following day I reintroduced the subject of body language and took everybody through what had happened in the bar the evening before, including the various examples of body language that I had witnessed from the rest of the group. My analysis of how each of them had felt, in some cases very annoyed, was so accurate that it was one of the best object lessons I have been able to use in proving that body language does work.

If they had any doubts before, they certainly believed it after that!

CHECKLIST – CHAPTER 10

■ Learn to understand the customer's body language.

■ Develop ways of handling problems which arise from that.

■ Develop ways of using the customer's body language to your advantage.

■ Learn how to use your own body language to advantage.

11

The thinking sales person

It seems a very long time ago that I wrote, and you read, in Chapter 1 that most people become involved in the sales profession without ever giving the selling process any real thought. Yet my personal experience of working with top sales people has been that they have indeed spent a great deal of time in thinking about the actual process which takes place.

So let us return to the theme of the Thinking Sales Person.

I know that I have emphasised that you are closing the sale from the minute you walk through the customer's door, but in reality it begins to happen even before that!

It happens when you decide on the type of company you want to target as a new prospect for your products and services. (If you read 'The Field Sales Handbook' which is published by Pitman in the same series as this you will see that I go into some detail about profiling customers and prospects.)

It happens when you conduct your research into who it is within that company that you ought to be meeting.

For many of you the quality of that research could be improved so let me give you some advice to help you once you are in the call and may be unsure about the quality of your contact.

When you find yourself in front of a customer your contact will fall into one of three categories:

1 The Paper Shuffler

This would only happen with a new prospect where you eventually recognise (hopefully sooner rather than later) that this person only processes the paperwork handed down from other people who have made decisions. The problem lies in getting them to hand you over to the real decision-makers, because they won't want to relinquish the illusion of power that their egos demand. In Chapter 9 I tried to give you some clues for identifying these people and some ideas about getting past them.

2 The MAN

This acronym means Money Authority and Need, and is the sales person's standard description for a decision-maker. This is someone you would definitely want to meet.

3 The AID

This acronym means the Ability to Influence the Decision. This level of contact isn't quite as good as the decision-maker, but is still someone you would want to meet. It may be that you enjoy better rapport with this contact and it may also be that in your business this is as high up the DMP as you can reasonably expect to go.

If you find it difficult to differentiate the MAN from the AID, the following may help. These are some of the classic factors that each will take into consideration when considering or recommending the purchase of any products or services.

The MAN will be interested in the following:

- Does what you are selling do the job that you promise?
- What return can be expected if I make the investment in this product or service?
- Do I need it?
- Conversely, can I do without it?
- Do I have money available to buy it?
- If I buy it, how will that affect the cash flow of the company?
- Is there another way to finance it?

- Will it enhance my company's image?
- Would buying it be in keeping with company policy?

If you recognise that these are the areas of interest you have certainly got the MAN or at least one of them, there could be more.

The AID will be interested in the following:

- How it works
- How it affects her or him
- Its reliability
- How safe it is
- How efficient it is
- How simple it is to use
- How easy it is to maintain.

157

This type of interest tells you that you are in discussion with the AID Don't despair; if it's appropriate in your business you may still be able to get to the MAN through the AID. In fact, it should be easier than trying to do so via the paper shuffler, because the AID still has enough influence not to feel threatened.

Some of these areas of interest will change depending on what it is that you are selling, for example, if you're selling advertising, then maintenance and simplicity of use wouldn't come into consideration, but there are clues in each of the areas of interest to help you to apply this thinking to your own personal situations.

When you have identified the MAN and the AID, it is extremely useful if you can get both together. If you achieve this you may find that while neither of them is against you there will usually be one who is more for you than the other. Be careful not to appear to push too heavily in that person's direction for fear that the other may think that he or she is being backed into a corner. It's very easy to direct your conversation at only one person in these meetings and it can be dangerous.

The next important part of 'closing the sale' before you even get to meet the customer is in the quality of your pre-call planning.

Pre-call planning

A fair amount is talked about pre-call planning, but my experience suggests that in the majority of cases, sales people – and indeed their managers – tend to make it up in the call as they go along. I call it 'busking' – it's not unlike the type of impromptu performance you would expect to see from a street entertainer, except it's invariably less professional than that. If you don't prepare in depth before you go into a call, don't be surprised if you come back out as empty-handed as you went in!

158

Many years ago one of my sales managers used to tell me that success in selling was ninety per cent perspiration and ten per cent inspiration and I still think that's pretty accurate.

There are three key things that you need to prepare before you go into the call to enhance your chances of success. I will outline them here, then expand upon them:

1   The **Main Objective** of the Call

2   The **Stages of Agreement**

3   The different **'Fall Back'** Positions.

The main objective is quite simple: 'what do I want to get out of this call?' The stages of agreement would be: 'what things do I need the customer to accept or agree upon so that I can build towards my main objective?' The 'fall back' positions would be: 'If I don't secure my main objective in this call, what will I ask for rather than come out empty-handed?'

Let's return to the Main Objective.

Most sales people I have met have a main objective in mind before they go into a meeting with a customer or prospect.

Surprisingly, that main objective isn't always as clear as it might be. It may be that their objective is to 'get an order'. It would be much better preparation to have a more clearly defined objective, for example, the exact type of order.

I meet sales people who insist that they go into meetings with the main objective of getting information from the customer or prospect. *That would only ever be a stage in the process!*

The real main objective would be the commitment from the customer to the next course of action based on that information. This could also include winning an order based on your sales presentation as a result of that information uncovering needs and desires. But it could in many instances be as simple as a return appointment.

You will often need information to be able to put together a proposal covering what you would provide, how long it would take or when it could be delivered and what the prices would be, based on all of that.

159

Therefore the real main objective in this situation would be to win commitment to a return appointment at which you would be able to make a presentation together with recommendations for action. Furthermore, at this stage you would also want to win commitment to doing business if your presentation and recommendations were found to be acceptable.

This is an important main objective for those of you who find yourself trying to oust a competitor, only to find that you are being used as a price checking service or that your proposals are being used so that the customer can squeeze a bit more out of his or her existing supplier. Other examples of main objectives would be any of the other stages of the selling process mentioned before, for example, tests, trials, factory visits, etc. In most cases, however, your main objective will be to make a specific sale.

Now we can look at the stages of agreement.

One of the stages could be the customer's agreement to give you the information in the first place. Another could be the agreement that your company would be found to be an acceptable supplier. Very few sales people that I have met have a really clear-cut idea of the stages they need to go through and the agreement they need to reach with the customer in order to build towards securing their main objective. Yet if you can't identify the various stages how can you possibly hope to win agreement to them?

Some of the obvious stages would include:

1   Acceptance of your quality of product or service.

2   Acceptance of your terms and conditions of contract.

3   Acceptance of your identification of needs and desires.

4   Acceptance that your product or service satisfies those needs and desires.

5   Where you are trying to replace an existing supplier, acceptance that the business is available to be won!

Having told you that many sales people have no clearly defined Main Objective or a clear-cut idea of the stages to which they need to secure agreement, I'm sure it comes as no surprise that I have found even fewer have any idea at all of what they should do in the event that they don't secure the main objective, albeit only at this meeting.

When this happens, the majority literally panic (remember the reaction to objections cartoon) and leave the meeting having secured nothing concrete, not even a return appointment. So I think we should look at what might be some of your 'fall back' positions, obviously dependent on the original main objective.

If we return to the situation which is most common, that of winning an order in the call, what would these 'fall backs' be if you didn't win the original order which was your main objective?

- Perhaps a smaller order, to be used as a trial?
- Perhaps agreement to the testing of some samples?

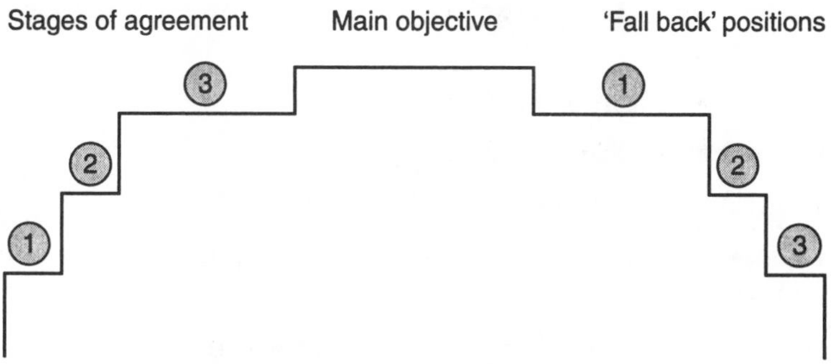

Fig 11.1 Pre-call planning

- Perhaps a meeting with some technical people to satisfy the customer that your product is up to the standard of specification required?
- Perhaps only the agreement to a further meeting to take your discussion to the next stage?

161

Whatever the 'fall back' positions, if you don't have them clear in your mind before you go in to the meeting, you may forget and come out having achieved little or nothing. I often work with sales people who are involved in a multiple call sale. There are quite a few businesses where this is the case, but I wonder how many times sales people create a multiple call sale where it isn't really necessary.

The following diagram will help you prepare for future sales calls.

Don't rely on your memory, complete one of these for each call – immediately before you go in, so that you don't forget in the heat of the moment.

Before, during and after the call, there are some questions you will also need to consider (you may even find a polite way of asking some of them) if you want to improve your chances of winning the business.

Evaluation questions

- Does the customer have the money?
- If not, can you offer the means to get the money?
- What are the customer's previous buying habits?
- Has the customer previously dealt successfully with either you or your company?
- Is this going to be a major decision for the customer?
- What about internal conflicts? for example, does someone in the company, who can influence the decision, have an otherwise 'vested interest'?
- What about the customer's priorities? for example, is there another financial demand conflicting with what you're trying to sell?
- Is the customer prepared to make some type of formal commitment? for example, a letter of intent, a purchase order number, written confirmation of a verbal agreement?
- Will the decision be influenced by timing or seasonal trends?
- Who else is competing for this business?
- How high is your contact level within the DMP?
- Will the decision be affected by outside market forces? for example, interest rates, government action, the weather, etc.
- How well have you identified the customer's needs? for example, why should he or she buy from **you**?
- How good is the quality of your proposal and your presentation?
- Is the customer a member of an influencing or buying group?
- Will it be all or nothing? that is could you get **some** of the business if you don't get it **all**?

The more of these questions that you can answer positively the better are your chances, but if you don't ask them, at least of yourself, your real probability of achieving success must be diminished.

I'm sure that there are some of you reading this book who are thinking that it's easier to write all this than it is to constantly do it.

You're right! It isn't so very long ago that I made the mistake of not taking one of these factors into consideration.

I worked for some years with the large Edinburgh-based Christian Salvesen Group. I received a call one day to ask if I would be interested in visiting one of their subsidiaries with a view to designing sales training for that business, which was certainly in an unusual field of operation and therefore unable to find an 'off the shelf' package that was suitable.

I arranged an appointment with the director responsible for this part of the company's operation and travelled to the head office for the meeting. I had what I thought was an extremely fruitful day. We had an open and honest discussion about the problems and I submitted my ideas for solving them. I left with a list of dates for carrying out the initial work, with the commitment from the customer that he would nominate the various people to be involved and notify me prior to the time. As the time drew near I had received no notification of the names of these people and had no success in having my calls returned. The project had died despite my high expectations! Some time later I had lunch with one of my main contacts in Salvesen's headquarters, MC (Mike) Barrie. Although he had not been the originator of the 'project' he was aware of what had happened and as I had worked very successfully with Mike for some time and he had been a real 'champion' of mine in his organisation and an absolute delight to work alongside, he was honest enough to give me his interpretation of what had taken place.

163

I had **assumed** that because I was dealing with a director of the board that he was the whole DMP and he wasn't. So on the odd occasion that you get it wrong don't become despondent. I am still getting it wrong and I've had the nerve to write the book!

The final type of preparation that I would like to tell you about here, can only be done after the call – but must be prepared for in advance.

Post-call analysis

Two things happen when you come out of a call:

1 You have won an order and are trying to get back to the car without showing too much delight to the customer.

2 You have failed to secure an order and as well as trying not to show too much disappointment, you're too shell-shocked to think what could have gone wrong!

The following diagram, which is an extension of the previous one, will help you analyse what went on in the call.

It isn't too uncommon for sales people to try to analyse what went wrong in sales calls, but it is extremely rare for them to take the time out to analyse what went right – particularly when an order was won.

So use this diagram to look at what happened regarding your stages, your main objective and your fall back positions, as well as thinking about the objections you met and how you handled them – or failed to handle them.

While all of the things that I have written in this section apply to normal 'one-to-one' selling situations, the need for the main objectives, stages of agreement and 'fall back' positions becomes even more important when selling to groups of people. As this is an ever increasing practice in the selling business, you may want to consider carrying out the same kind of preparation for when you find yourself in those situations. Only carry it out in even more detail. *The Field Sales Handbook* addresses the subject of selling to groups in more detail than I have time for here.

Stages of agreement   Main objective   'Fall back' positions

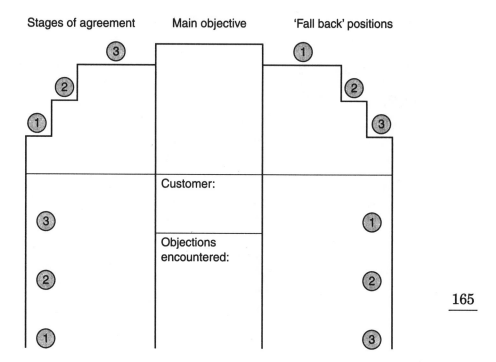

Fig 11.2 Post-call analysis

CHECKLIST – CHAPTER 11

■ Identify the paper shufflers – and bypass them.

■ Identify the MAN and the AID and treat them accordingly.

■ Carry out real quality pre-call planning:
  – have clearly identified main objectives,
  – clear-cut stages of agreement,
  – 'fall back' positions defined in advance.

■ Ask yourself the evaluation questions.

■ Conduct in depth post-call analysis – even when you've won the order.

166

12

How to get to the top

If you have read this far through the book you have certainly displayed the type of tenacity that you will need to get to the top. If you merely skipped through and are reading this chapter first, I hope that what follows will encourage you to go back and read the rest. If on the other hand you have read through this book having already read *The Field Sales Handbook* then in addition to your tenacity, your patience, determination and stamina are also to be admired!

Step one: insist on training!

It's not negotiable. Much of the responsibility is yours but there must be a significant effort on the part of the company for whom you work. Make them face up to that responsibility – and if they won't, LEAVE!

There are companies out there who still invest in training. I use the word invest advisedly because training is a genuine investment despite the fact that the accountancy profession insists on putting training on the income statement as a cost. All of the major companies who make a significant investment in training have also measured the return on the investment. Only an investment gives you a return.

But you wouldn't expect me to say anything else in my business would you? I'm not beating the drum to solicit more business; I'm talking about all kinds of training, not just my speciality areas. Look at what has happened not only in the UK and Europe in recent years but throughout the western world. The skills base has become eroded to the point where, if there was a significant upturn in the fate of the major economic powers, it's arguable whether or not they would have the ability to handle it.

Consider periods of recession. Almost without exception, the financial 'axe' falls in the following order:

1   Training is either cut back or cut out all together.

2   Advertising and other parts of the marketing budget are cut.

3   Research and development budgets are cut.

4   Manufacturing investment is cut back or suspended.

5   Graduate recruitment is cut back or in some cases suspended.

6   Other recruitment is suspended.

7   The labour force: management, clerical and shop floor, is reduced.

Don't get confused; this book is not about politics, it's about excellence!

If you want to get to the top, work for the type of company that doesn't run for cover and cut the training budget as soon as the going gets tough! The good companies are out there – look for them, they will welcome someone with your determination.

There is a worse example, however, than companies who cut back on training and that's the companies who never did it in the first place. I even have to listen to garbage like, 'If we train our people we only make it attractive for our competition to try to recruit them!' Honest, they're being serious. Don't go to work for them unless you want to slide into an abyss of mediocrity.

How any company can fail to recognise the benefits of training is beyond me. Look at the changes that you experience on a day-to-day basis which have nothing to do with your profession. Does anybody get any quality of service anymore? Yes, from businesses that are renowned for their training policies and practices or from small businesses that are still run by the owners, but only from these. Have you tried cashing a cheque at a high street bank lately? Everybody is so busy 'mugging' you to buy insurance, pensions, investments and the like, or loans for this and loans for that, that there aren't any people left to take care of simple transactions like cashing cheques. If there's no commission in it, move over and make way for the next customer who may be more amenable to the approach. I talk to the staff in banks, actually I talk to anybody, and they tell me that they haven't been trained to carry out this new function but they are still expected to try to do it! They don't have to tell me that they haven't been trained, I'm in the business where I can tell within minutes whether they have or not and whether the training was effective.

169

How can people manage change if they haven't had the training? Let me come back to sales people. You may be working for the type of company that carries out induction training with every new member of sales staff and therefore assume that all companies do the same. Let me assure you that some of the biggest names in business are still handing brochures and car keys to sales people on their first day on the job and telling them that they won't sell anything sitting in the office so get out there!

In reality, immeasurable damage is done in these situations because the poor sales person is likely to destroy some good prospective business without the proper training. It would be more profitable to refuse to let them talk to potential customers than to let them run around loose. Even if you have had selling experience, on your first day you don't have the depth of product knowledge to make sure that you don't ruin a good opportunity!

OK, I'll shut up now, I think I may have got the message across.

Step two: mentoring

The dictionary describes a mentor as a wise or trusted advisor or guide. This means that it must be someone you know intimately! You may very well decide to model yourself on someone, or the particular attributes of someone, but a mentor is an entirely different being.

Get yourself a mentor who will advise and guide you through your career. You may find, like me, that you outgrow some of these but pupil turned teacher was always a good road to travel!

Become a mentor to other people!

Let me tell you that being someone else's trusted advisor or guide is an awesome responsibility which will develop you as much as the person you are advising!

170

Step three: practice

Whether you are being trained by your company or not, retrain yourself with constant practice. If it's good enough for the world's top golfers to constantly practice I would think that it's good enough for you. Sales people tell me that they don't know how to practice other than in front of the customer. Of course they do; it's called a role play! Sales people also tell me that they don't like carrying out role plays because it's so false. It isn't the falseness that they don't like it's the fear of making a fool of themselves in front of their peer group. The wonderful thing about role playing is that you get the chance to practice without losing any customers.

Gather together a group of two other colleagues, making three including yourself, and create role play situations. You will each take turns at being the customer, the sales person and the observer, who can give objective feedback. Each of you should prepare a real life situation from your own business, either one in which you are currently involved or have recently been involved (whether the outcome was successful or not). You will each play the part of your own customer and will give whoever plays the part of the sales person some background information, without giving away the types of objection that you met, or would anticipate meeting.

To help you carry this out as successfully as possible I have provided below some guidelines for each role.

The Sales Person

Your job is to conduct the sales call using all of the techniques described in this book, paying particular attention to 'Digging for Gold', the objection handling technique and the closing techniques.

171

The Customer

Remind the sales person briefly who you are playing. Don't be too awkward but on the other hand don't be a pushover. When you hear open questions give these good answers with lots of information. When you hear closed questions that are inappropriate at the time, give them one word YES or NO answers.

The Observer

Your role is really the most important as you will be able to be objective whereas your colleagues will be too tied up in the role play to notice as much as you will. Look for the following:

- Did the sales person cover all of the steps of the sale?
- How good was the personal and company introduction?
- How clearly was the objective of the meeting stated?
- Did the sales person get the customer to want to answer questions or was it straight in at the deep end?
- How good were the open questions?

- How well was 'Digging for Gold' used and how well were the answers used to control the direction of the conversation?
- What needs and desires were uncovered and what other 'nuggets' were used?
- How well did the sales person use the various selling aids, including the features and benefits analyses, etc.?
- How good and accurate was the summary?
- Did the sales person ask, 'Is there anything else?'
- Did the sales person use the $64 000 question?

Make notes as the role play progresses and be prepared to offer a commentary at the end. Don't be too critical (it could be your turn next) but don't be too soft either. Try to use examples to highlight your points. Practise with your friends and colleagues in this manner and you will be astonished at the improvement in your performance!

Step four: personal and career development

The final area I would like to address with regard to getting to the top, is your own **personal and career development.**

The first thing you have to do is analyse your current qualifications, that is, the areas of knowledge and skill that are needed to successfully do the job.

I have provided a list of some of the subjects that ought to be included, based on my work with some of my own clients, but this is not exhaustive. You will need to develop your own list relating to your business and perhaps you may elicit the help of a manager or colleague in putting this list together.

Let's begin with the Knowledge Areas (see Fig 12.1).

If you look at the area that refers to the range of products/services, you may have to break these further down into specific groups. Similarly, in the area that refers to knowl-

AREAS OF KNOWLEDGE

Knowledge of your own company:

The structure of the company	1 2 3 4 5 6 7 8 9 10 11 12 13 14 15 16 17 18 19 20
The history of the company	1 2 3 4 5 6 7 8 9 10 11 12 13 14 15 16 17 18 19 20
The corporate objectives	1 2 3 4 5 6 7 8 9 10 11 12 13 14 15 16 17 18 19 20
The product strategies	1 2 3 4 5 6 7 8 9 10 11 12 13 14 15 16 17 18 19 20
New product development	1 2 3 4 5 6 7 8 9 10 11 12 13 14 15 16 17 18 19 20
The company's share of the market	1 2 3 4 5 6 7 8 9 10 11 12 13 14 15 16 17 18 19 20

Knowledge of the products/services:

The range of products/services	1 2 3 4 5 6 7 8 9 10 11 12 13 14 15 16 17 18 19 20
How the products work	1 2 3 4 5 6 7 8 9 10 11 12 13 14 15 16 17 18 19 20
How they are made	1 2 3 4 5 6 7 8 9 10 11 12 13 14 15 16 17 18 19 20
The materials and design	1 2 3 4 5 6 7 8 9 10 11 12 13 14 15 16 17 18 19 20
Their position against the competition	1 2 3 4 5 6 7 8 9 10 11 12 13 14 15 16 17 18 19 20
The pricing structure	1 2 3 4 5 6 7 8 9 10 11 12 13 14 15 16 17 18 19 20
The sales terms	1 2 3 4 5 6 7 8 9 10 11 12 13 14 15 16 17 18 19 20
The warranty conditions	1 2 3 4 5 6 7 8 9 10 11 12 13 14 15 16 17 18 19 20
The service terms	1 2 3 4 5 6 7 8 9 10 11 12 13 14 15 16 17 18 19 20

Knowledge of the market:

The size of the market	1 2 3 4 5 6 7 8 9 10 11 12 13 14 15 16 17 18 19 20
The trends in the market	1 2 3 4 5 6 7 8 9 10 11 12 13 14 15 16 17 18 19 20
The customer profile	1 2 3 4 5 6 7 8 9 10 11 12 13 14 15 16 17 18 19 20
Environmental forces	1 2 3 4 5 6 7 8 9 10 11 12 13 14 15 16 17 18 19 20
Government regulations	1 2 3 4 5 6 7 8 9 10 11 12 13 14 15 16 17 18 19 20

Knowledge of your own customers:

The buying policy	1 2 3 4 5 6 7 8 9 10 11 12 13 14 15 16 17 18 19 20
The Decision Making Process	1 2 3 4 5 6 7 8 9 10 11 12 13 14 15 16 17 18 19 20
Buying patterns	1 2 3 4 5 6 7 8 9 10 11 12 13 14 15 16 17 18 19 20
Affiliations to other companies or buying groups	1 2 3 4 5 6 7 8 9 10 11 12 13 14 15 16 17 18 19 20
Terms and conditions of contract	1 2 3 4 5 6 7 8 9 10 11 12 13 14 15 16 17 18 19 20

Knowledge of your competitors:

The ownership (part of a group)	1 2 3 4 5 6 7 8 9 10 11 12 13 14 15 16 17 18 19 20
The product range	1 2 3 4 5 6 7 8 9 10 11 12 13 14 15 16 17 18 19 20
Strengths or weaknesses of the products	1 2 3 4 5 6 7 8 9 10 11 12 13 14 15 16 17 18 19 20
Strengths or weaknesses of the pricing policies	1 2 3 4 5 6 7 8 9 10 11 12 13 14 15 16 17 18 19 20
Their penetration with your customers	1 2 3 4 5 6 7 8 9 10 11 12 13 14 15 16 17 18 19 20
Their core business	1 2 3 4 5 6 7 8 9 10 11 12 13 14 15 16 17 18 19 20

173

Fig 12.1 Personal development profile

edge of your competitors, you may want to add some items in addition to the questions I have asked.

Now look at the predominantly skill areas;

If you are a sales manager reading this section, there is a supplement that has been designed especially for you (see Figs 12.2 and 12.3).

When you have finalised your list of knowledge and skill areas, rate yourself on a scale of 1 to 20, 20 being excellence bordering on perfection.

AREAS OF SKILL

Telephone appointment making:

Overcoming objections	1 2 3 4 5 6 7 8 9 10 11 12 13 14 15 16 17 18 19 20
Closing techniques	1 2 3 4 5 6 7 8 9 10 11 12 13 14 15 16 17 18 19 20

Selling skills when 'face-to-face':

Your own and company introduction	1 2 3 4 5 6 7 8 9 10 11 12 13 14 15 16 17 18 19 20
Establishing the DMP	1 2 3 4 5 6 7 8 9 10 11 12 13 14 15 16 17 18 19 20
Questioning skills	1 2 3 4 5 6 7 8 9 10 11 12 13 14 15 16 17 18 19 20
Note taking	1 2 3 4 5 6 7 8 9 10 11 12 13 14 15 16 17 18 19 20
Other information gathering skills	1 2 3 4 5 6 7 8 9 10 11 12 13 14 15 16 17 18 19 20
Identifiying needs and desires	1 2 3 4 5 6 7 8 9 10 11 12 13 14 15 16 17 18 19 20
Summarising	1 2 3 4 5 6 7 8 9 10 11 12 13 14 15 16 17 18 19 20
Presenting your recommendations	1 2 3 4 5 6 7 8 9 10 11 12 13 14 15 16 17 18 19 20
Presenting price	1 2 3 4 5 6 7 8 9 10 11 12 13 14 15 16 17 18 19 20
Handling objections	1 2 3 4 5 6 7 8 9 10 11 12 13 14 15 16 17 18 19 20
Closing the sale	1 2 3 4 5 6 7 8 9 10 11 12 13 14 15 16 17 18 19 20
Winning commitment to the next stage	1 2 3 4 5 6 7 8 9 10 11 12 13 14 15 16 17 18 19 20
Keeping control	1 2 3 4 5 6 7 8 9 10 11 12 13 14 15 16 17 18 19 20
Body language	1 2 3 4 5 6 7 8 9 10 11 12 13 14 15 16 17 18 19 20
Presenting to groups	1 2 3 4 5 6 7 8 9 10 11 12 13 14 15 16 17 18 19 20
Establishing rapport	1 2 3 4 5 6 7 8 9 10 11 12 13 14 15 16 17 18 19 20

Other areas of knowledge and skill:

Knowledge of your own area	1 2 3 4 5 6 7 8 9 10 11 12 13 14 15 16 17 18 19 20
Territory management	1 2 3 4 5 6 7 8 9 10 11 12 13 14 15 16 17 18 19 20
Letter and proposal writing	1 2 3 4 5 6 7 8 9 10 11 12 13 14 15 16 17 18 19 20
Report writing	1 2 3 4 5 6 7 8 9 10 11 12 13 14 15 16 17 18 19 20
Personal administration	1 2 3 4 5 6 7 8 9 10 11 12 13 14 15 16 17 18 19 20
Pre-call planning	1 2 3 4 5 6 7 8 9 10 11 12 13 14 15 16 17 18 19 20
Cyclical call planning	1 2 3 4 5 6 7 8 9 10 11 12 13 14 15 16 17 18 19 20

Fig 12.2 Personal development profile

The next thing you may have to do is try to be objective and rate each of the items on the basis of the levels demanded by the job.

There is one thing I would like you to make special note of: the situation where your qualifications are already in excess of that demanded by the job. This is usually an area where you are particularly comfortable. Beware that in these situations you may indulge yourself in too much of that type of activity at the expense of something more important.

One of the classics which springs to mind is report writing. Sales people hate paperwork, so whenever I come across a sales person who enjoys, and is therefore good at, paperwork, I find that at times when they are under pressure, they have a tendency to hide themselves in it. It doesn't mean that if you do enjoy paperwork this will happen, but it is worth watching for.

175

Select the three or four areas where the difference between what is needed and what exists is greatest and create a **personal development plan**.

MANAGEMENT AREAS OF KNOWLEDGE AND SKILL

Team leadership	1 2 3 4 5 6 7 8 9 10 11 12 13 14 15 16 17 18 19 20
Decision making	1 2 3 4 5 6 7 8 9 10 11 12 13 14 15 16 17 18 19 20
Problem solving	1 2 3 4 5 6 7 8 9 10 11 12 13 14 15 16 17 18 19 20
Coaching	1 2 3 4 5 6 7 8 9 10 11 12 13 14 15 16 17 18 19 20
Counselling	1 2 3 4 5 6 7 8 9 10 11 12 13 14 15 16 17 18 19 20
Performance appraisal	1 2 3 4 5 6 7 8 9 10 11 12 13 14 15 16 17 18 19 20
Conducting field accompaniment	1 2 3 4 5 6 7 8 9 10 11 12 13 14 15 16 17 18 19 20
Training in the classroom	1 2 3 4 5 6 7 8 9 10 11 12 13 14 15 16 17 18 19 20
Running effective sales meetings	1 2 3 4 5 6 7 8 9 10 11 12 13 14 15 16 17 18 19 20
Objective setting	1 2 3 4 5 6 7 8 9 10 11 12 13 14 15 16 17 18 19 20
Exhibition management	1 2 3 4 5 6 7 8 9 10 11 12 13 14 15 16 17 18 19 20
Financial awareness	1 2 3 4 5 6 7 8 9 10 11 12 13 14 15 16 17 18 19 20
Budgeting, targeting and forecasting	1 2 3 4 5 6 7 8 9 10 11 12 13 14 15 16 17 18 19 20
Recruitment and induction of sales people	1 2 3 4 5 6 7 8 9 10 11 12 13 14 15 16 17 18 19 20
Inter-departmental communication	1 2 3 4 5 6 7 8 9 10 11 12 13 14 15 16 17 18 19 20
Account management	1 2 3 4 5 6 7 8 9 10 11 12 13 14 15 16 17 18 19 20
Stress management-in your team*	1 2 3 4 5 6 7 8 9 10 11 12 13 14 15 16 17 18 19 20

Fig 12.3 Supplement for managers

The time scale for the 'from' and 'to' should be six months. Thereafter you will be able to create a rolling six month development plan. Limit the number of areas to three or four otherwise you won't be able to complete the plan and continue bringing in the results.

When you have written the areas for development on the plan, consider what you may have to do to bring about the Achievement:

■ Study some books?

■ Attend a training course?

■ Work with a colleague? etc.

Now consider the resource that you may have to call on:

■ Will your company send you on a course?

■ Do they have a distance-learning library?

Personal development plan   From   To

Area for development	Action for achievement	Resource	Start date	Review date	Standard desired

Fig 12.4 Personal development plan

■ Can you find what you're looking for in a public library?

Reading books is great, but it's only part of the solution. There is no substitute for training being carried out in an environment where ideas can be shared or even challenged, where someone can demonstrate the skills and explain the finer points of ideas.

Similarly, on the job training is vital, where a colleague or manager can show by example or can observe you in action to be able to give you feedback on how well you are developing.

Now set a start date for each activity, making them different start dates within the six-month period. Set a review date when you will check your progress. Make a note of the current standard and the one you wish to achieve during the time allowed. Remember not to expect too much. If you chose an area where your level is 11, don't expect to move from 11 to 18 in one step. Create stages and aim for 14 as a first step. On your second six-month plan you will be able to aim for the next improvement.

177

When all of this has been done, make a copy of your personal development plan and give that copy to someone very close to you. The reason is simple, you need to know that someone else will recognise if you have broken a promise you made to yourself!

In my supplement for managers, you may have noticed that I put an asterisk beside the item 'Stress Management – in your Team'. The reason for this is that recent research suggests that there are a number of people who actually thrive on stress and that these can usually be found at the top in their chosen profession. If that is the case, perhaps it is more important for a manager to consider the various things which cause stress in her or his people. Good management practice can reduce the incidence of stress in people, so I have concentrated here on that aspect of stress management rather than on addressing it in the manager.

Step five: the psychology of success

To make this work to maximum effect, you will need to begin by taking some note paper and carrying out some self analysis.

Here is a short exercise for you:

1 List THREE Goals you have set and achieved in the past. Anyone who has a Professional Qualification or a University Degree etc., will be immediately able to identify at least one. Don't give up at one, if you're old enough to be in selling, you will have achieved at least three, perhaps including getting your current job.

2 List your THREE Most Important Career Goals – at this moment. It could be promotion, or a change of job or being top sales person. If you want to be successful, you will have them!

3 List your THREE Most Important Personal or Family Goals – at this moment. Remember that it's very easy when you're concentrating on business to forget that you have a family – DON'T.

4 List your THREE Most Important Financial Goals – at this moment. Perhaps you want to buy a new car, have a special holiday or buy a new house.

5 If it was possible to guarantee success in any one endeavour – what would it be? *Note*: Goals or objectives are measurable, achievable and time oriented.

6 Name THREE people at the top of your field right now – then list what you think you could learn from them. There are people at the top of every profession – to be successful you should know who they are.

7 Make a note of what you are currently doing about number 6 above.

8 Make a list of the business, management or 'technical' magazines or books which you actively seek out and study – even if you only study parts of them.

9 How many books do you read – on average –
  - per year?
  - per month?
  - per week?

10 Of these, how many are fiction and how many non-fiction?

11 What made you decide to get into the selling business?

12 Is what you do for a living the most fun you can have with your clothes on?

13 If not, what would you rather be doing for a living?

14 If you have answered NO to number 12 above and have been able to give an answer to number 13 what positive steps can you take to bring this about?

179

I said at the beginning of the exercise that it was a short one. However, if you spent any less than half an hour on it, you didn't think deeply enough – or maybe your desire to be successful isn't as great as you thought it was? If the point of some of my questions in that exercise wasn't clear, it soon should be.

I would now like to give you my 'Ten-Point Plan for Success'! Remember, however, irrespective of your personal definition of success: **Your ultimate aim is to be happy and fulfilled!**

1 You will need to develop self-discipline to achieve everything you want in your career

Don't follow the 'line of least resistance' – discipline is the cornerstone of success.

2 Make sure that you have purpose in your life

Set yourself meaningful, stretching goals. First; **decide what you want** from your career. Then, **determine the price that you will have to pay.** This price isn't necessarily in monetary terms, it is more likely to be the time and effort you will need to devote to achieving what you want. It will also include sacrificing some of the things that you enjoy – albeit short term. Finally, you then have to **commit to paying the price** – otherwise it won't work.

I always found that a bit of 'backward planning' helped me. If you can determine what it is you want, you can usually work backwards to identify what it is that you have to do to get it.

3 Strive for excellence

Try to be the best at what you do. Use successful people you know as role models – or at worst try to learn from the mistakes of others. Surround yourself with successful people. Read their books. There's a wonderful American expression which goes: 'Don't mix with the turkeys – fly with the eagles!' In *Up the Organisation* , Robert Townsend says, 'If you can't do it excellently, don't do it at all. Because if it's not excellent it won't be profitable or fun, and if you're not in business for fun or profit, what the hell are you doing here?'

The real secret of success is: find what you like doing best – then find someone who'll pay you for doing it!

4 Hold yourself responsible for your own success

Don't blame other people if things don't go right. Stop making excuses to yourself! Get rid of this notion of luck! Believe me, the harder and smarter you work the luckier you will become.

5 Concentrate on your self development – the responsibility is yours

On a daily basis I come across people who think that because their formal education is complete they have learned all that they need to.

I have a simple test for anyone who wants to know if their learning is complete. Hold a mirror in front of your mouth and if the mirror mists up because you're breathing – your learning hasn't yet finished! In all of my career I have discovered among the top people in industry and commerce that I have met, that there is one thing they all have in common; quite simply – they know more than the rest of us!

6 Practice creativity

I often refer to the creativity of sales peoples' call reports and expenses claims, this isn't what I mean here. Work on the principle that there is a better way of doing things than at present and constantly be looking for that better way. You only need to be a little better than your competition to be considerably more successful. Don't subscribe to the school of mediocrity that believes: 'If it isn't broken – don't fix it!'

7 Don't give up – there will be setbacks

If it was easy everyone would be doing it – which would probably cause you to redefine the criteria for success. So have courage and be persistent.

8 Work and co-operate with others

You won't be able to do it entirely alone. You will need help and co-operation from your loved ones and your colleagues.

9 Have integrity and be honest

Edward De Bono, in his book, *Tactics, The Art and Science of Success,* quotes Lord Forté, who founded the Trust House Forte Hotel and Catering Chain (THF), as saying, 'You must be able to go anywhere in the world and know there'll be no one there who can point a finger and say – that man did me down!' I'm sure that all of you reading this book can identify successful people you know, whose success is not begrudged by others while at the same time you will know successful people whose demise is anticipated with glee. If you don't practice honesty and integrity in your dealings with people, it won't be a question of them awaiting your downfall, they will be trying to help you fall all the way – and you'll deserve it! Business history, much of it recent, is littered with many deserving cases of 'come-uppance'.

10 Be single-minded

You have to concentrate on the achievement of your own success. However, don't confuse single-mindedness with selfishness. That is as valid as confusing assertiveness with aggression.

Let me leave you with a couple of additional thoughts: My good friend Derek Stables, who retired recently as Director of Management Education and Training for Ciba-Geigy plc, used to say: 'The ONLY place where SUCCESS comes before WORK – is in a Dictionary!'

From my own observations let me tell you that there are only **four types of people**:

- Those who **make things happen**,
- Those who **watch things happen**,
- Those who **wonder what happened**, and
- Those who are blissfully **unaware that anything ever did happen**.

The reason I asked you in one of the self-evaluation exercises if you found selling the most fun you could have with your clothes on is quite simple. If you didn't answer positively, maybe you should think again.

This is a really tough business when you enjoy it. It will be sheer hell if you don't!

This entire chapter has been devoted, one way or another, to success achieved through hard work, professionalism, dedication, integrity, honesty and excellence in everything that you do. I think it is appropriate, therefore, to end this final chapter with a story about Robin Terrell, the Group Vice President of Ciba Vision, who featured as far back as the introduction, who was ultimately responsible for giving the book its title and who is the epitome of each and every one of those virtues mentioned.

When I began working with Robin he was the Managing Director of Ciba Vision in the UK. We formulated a quality programme which we called 'The Journey to Excellence' during which a number of three-day, two-day and one-day seminars were organised to be run at every level in the company. We began with the senior management team and created a vision and a mission statement. During the course of the programme, Robin had committed to delivering that vision and mission statement to every member of his workforce. About halfway through 'The Journey to Excellence' programme, we had a chat at the end of a week in which we had been running the one-day seminars and I told Robin that I had recently taken delivery of the new Tom Peter's video, *'The Tom Peter's Experience – The Customer Revolution'* produced by BBC Training Videos and that I would let him see it when I returned the following week. When the time for the next seminar came round, Robin had been called away to attend a meeting in Switzerland and had asked his personnel manager to deputise for him. He returned later that evening, after the seminar, and I told him that I was really keen to show him the new video although there was a part of the film that I thought he may not like. I can't remember if it was later that evening or early the next morning but it was certainly before the seminar scheduled for the next day that I showed him the film.

183

In his film, Tom Peters talks about the ten traits involved in a quality revolution and when he gets to number nine he tells how he believes that the quality programme will fail within eighteen months. He points out that companies launch quality programmes and then set up a series of recognition programmes to be run perhaps on a monthly basis. On the first recognition programme the chairman, managing director and senior officers of the company attend, as they do on the second and the third and on the fourth. The fifth programme comes around and there is a budget crisis, a competitor crisis or a 'raider' crisis. The chairman or managing director can't quite make that one but others will go. He goes on to say that on the day of that decision you can 'kiss your quality programme' good-bye.

You can obviously understand my reticence at showing that part of the film in the light of what had happened.

The following day, Robin appeared in order to deliver his vision and mission statement to the group and began by telling them that he owed both them and their colleagues an apology for not being present the previous day and that as a result of his absence I had 'chastised' him. He went on to promise that he wouldn't miss another and promised to make sure that everyone who had been present the previous day would receive his apology. He kept his promise not only about the apology but also about his future presence.

I don't know what words you might use to describe that, but among the ones that immediately spring to my mind are:

- Professionalism
- Dedication
- Integrity
- Honesty
- Excellence.

CHECKLIST – CHAPTER 12

- Insist on training and if you don't get it, go somewhere else where you will get it!

- Get yourself a mentor and in the fullness of time – become someone else's mentor!

- Practice – until you drop!

- Analyse, honestly, your qualifications and create a personal development plan.

- Concentrate on your own career development.

- Develop the psychology of success!

185

Conclusion

■

I began this book by telling you that I decided to write it to redress the balance between the plethora of books that have been written over the years outlining the WHATS of selling and the minimal number, if any, that have been written about the HOWS. Having read the book and used it as a training manual and worked your way through it, I hope you think that I achieved my objective. I also hope that you found that some of my real-life experiences brightened up what could have been extremely dry subject matter. I had originally intended to include many more of these, but as I read through what had been written I began to feel that too many stories could have trivialised the book.

That the business of selling is an honourable profession is a conviction that I hold with a passion that none who have worked with me would doubt for a moment. Therefore I didn't want the seriousness of my message to be at risk.

When I began to write the book I thought that I would end up with a piece of work which was entirely about selling and sales people, but now that it has been completed I have come to believe that it is as much about excellence as it is about anything else. In this case it is about the potential excellence of you – the amazing band of people who keep the economies of the world afloat – sales people. Whether you are known as 'reps', sales executives, area sales managers, account managers or any of the other titles that are bestowed upon you, a basic fact of life is that if you weren't out there selling, the world as we know it would come to a grinding halt.

I congratulate you on finishing the book and would like to refer you back to the very last chapter which was devoted to showing you how to get to the top of your profession.

I would not be so arrogant as to suggest that I have come even close to reaching that stage yet, but the fact that I have been able to write this book is in no small measure due to the many people who have had a profound influence on me over the years, sometimes without knowing it. I feel, therefore, that they have earned the right to be mentioned here.

Jim McIntyre with whom I worked in Babcock Power who was certainly my first mentor.

Peter Chamberlain at Rank Xerox who showed me that selling can be a fun business too, until his career advancement broke up the team!

Douglas Martyn, now the Chief Executive of Scottish Innovation, with whom I also worked at Rank Xerox, who showed me that I had to find a method that worked for me and that I couldn't succeed by trying to be something I wasn't.

AC (Fred) Will, retired senior manager with Esso and also a retired director of Scottish Innovation whose sheer dedication and professionalism in everything that he does – including his water colour paintings – is an object lesson.

Peter Jensen, Chairman and Senior Vice President of SmithKline Beecham Consumer Health Care in Europe, who as well as being an outstanding example of professionalism has totally redefined **enthusiasm** for me.

Rod Leaver, Managing Director of Laurentian Financial Advisers, with whom I worked and did business when he was Sales Director of Commercial Union Financial Services, who has delighted me with his professional and totally pragmatic approach to business.

Derek Stables, retired Director of Management Education and Training for Ciba Geigy plc. A real training 'pro' who helped me in my business and with whom I shared a lot of laughter and sadly a few tears.

Neil Craig, the Deputy MD of Ciba Pigments who is as astute a businessman as I have ever met and the first accountant I ever knew who had a sense of humour.

Nick Hawkins, the chief accountant of the Clayton Aniline Company, the second accountant I met with a sense of humour and the first one to demonstrate to me a real commitment to investment in training.

Robin Terrell, the Group Vice President of Ciba Vision. He has featured so prominently in this book that I really can't say any more without causing him embarrassment, but I refuse to make my list of ten without including him.

These are the 'good guys' who have taught me a great deal and I could have made the list longer, so if anyone has been missed who knows they ought to be here I hope you will understand that I needed to leave some room for you in the next book.

189

Let me end as I began:

If you have really studied this book you now have the ability to live up to the title and become your company's ULTIMATE USP.

Bibliography

■

Up The Organisation by Robert Townsend (Hodder Fawcett, 1971)

In Search of Excellence by Thomas J Peters and Robert H Waterman Jr. (Harper & Row, 1982)

Tactics: The Art and Science of Success by Edward De Bono (Harper Collins, 1986)

Thriving on Chaos by Tom Peters (Macmillan Publishing, 1988)

The Tom Peters Experience: The Customer Revolution by Tom Peters (video film, BBC Training Videos, 1989)

Pricing for Results by John Winkler (Heinemann Professional Publishing, 1991)

The Field Sales Handbook by Jim Cowden (Pitman Publishing, 1994)

Index

■

193